Praise

"At a time when pessimism seems to be the watchword on the African continent, *Afro-Optimism Unleashed* is a must-read for African entrepreneurs aspiring to make a global impact, and for anyone doing business in Africa. From its inspiring stories and practical advice to its emphasis on building strong networks and cultivating a global mindset, this book offers a comprehensive roadmap for success on the continent. Whether you're just starting out or looking to scale your existing business, *Afro-Optimism Unleashed* provides invaluable insights and strategies that will help you achieve your goals."

—**Andrew Alli**, Investor and Business Adviser (Africa)

"Reading *Afro-Optimism Unleashed* was a real enlightenment for me as a leader, and I believe it will be for anyone shaping Africa's future. This isn't just another book on business strategy; it's a guide filled with principles and policies that drive African excellence in leadership, business, and innovation. Adeolu's ability to blend global perspectives with the realities of African entrepreneurship gave me a fresh perspective on my own work. Her call to root our businesses in a local context while embracing a global vision is exactly the wisdom the next generation of leaders need. This book isn't just theory – it's actionable, inspiring, and a true navigator for African entrepreneurial success."

> — **Bode Pedro**, Founder and Chief Executive Officer, Casava (Nigeria)

"Afro-Optimism Unleashed is a must-read for any African entrepreneur aspiring to make a global impact. Adeolu's insights on cultivating a global mindset and building strong networks are invaluable. The practical guidance and real-world examples make this book both inspiring and actionable. I highly recommend it to anyone looking to scale their vision and achieve sustainable success."

> — **Derrick Edem Akpalu, PhD**, Chief Executive Officer and Co-founder, Revna Biosciences (Ghana)

"Afro-Optimism Unleashed was a refreshing read, even for a non-native English speaker like me. It's well-structured and full of engaging stories and practical insights. It definitely refueled my commitment to the development of our communities and making a positive impact on people's lives. I highly recommend it to African business leaders and anyone considering returning to Africa. It's a

valuable resource for navigating and transforming the challenges into opportunities for the continent."

— **Ibrahim Coulibaly**, Managing Director, Finafrica Assurances (Senegal)

"I loved reading *Afro-Optimism Unleashed*! Adeolu's practical tools and actionable advice are invaluable for entrepreneurs looking to scale their vision. Overall, this is a fantastic book that offers a wealth of insights for aspiring entrepreneurs."

— **Kanini Mutooni**, Regional Managing Director, Africa, Draper Richards Kaplan Foundation (Kenya)

"*Afro-Optimism Unleashed* is a competent and trustworthy read. Adeolu's upbeat and enthusiastic style makes the complex topics accessible and relatable. Her insights and guidance are valuable for visionaries who are seeking success. I simply enjoyed the journey. Highly recommended!"

— **Marsha Wulff**, Co-founder, LoftyInc Capital (USA)

"*Afro-Optimism Unleashed* is a breath of fresh air! It's an easy read with practical advice that I can apply immediately. I initially thought it was targeted toward those returning to Africa, but I quickly realized it's about leadership in any context. The real-life narratives and relatable examples made me feel less alone in my journey as an Afro-optimist. I highly recommend this book to anyone looking to scale their vision and make a global impact."

— **Sylvester Nzioka**, Chief Operating Officer and Principal Officer, Jubilee Allianz General Insurance Kenya Limited (Kenya)

"*Afro-Optimism Unleashed* is an essential read for anyone serious about scaling their business and achieving long-term success. It's packed with powerful insights and presented in a way that's both accessible and engaging. The emphasis on trust and assembling the right team really stands out. Adeolu's work has been invaluable to me, and I'm grateful to have her as a business partner. I highly recommend this book to anyone aiming to make meaningful impact on a global scale."

— **Tiekie Barnard**, Chief Executive Officer, Shift Impact Africa and Shared Value Africa (South Africa)

AFRO-OPTIMISM UNLEASHED

SCALING AFRICAN EXCELLENCE TO THE GLOBAL STAGE

ADEOLU ADEWUMI-ZER

WITH CONTRIBUTIONS FROM
SEUN OSHUNKOYA AND MATTHEW NASH
OF WESTWOOD INVESTMENT CONSULTANCY

Rᵉthink

First published in Great Britain in 2025
by Rethink Press (www.rethinkpress.com)

Cover image © Shutterstock | Ketmut, Nature Peaceful and shuttersv

For Mommy, Grace Ibilola Adewumi nee Sangodeyi.

My journey of resilience began with you.

Contents

Foreword

Afro-optimism is alive and well in Africa, and it's the driving force behind the continent's potential for greatness. During the eight years that I worked across all regions of Africa, including seven years as regional CEO for Allianz and serving on nine African boards, I witnessed firsthand the incredible talent and opportunities that abound in this region.

Adeolu Adewumi-Zer embodies the spirit of Afro-optimism in a very personal way in her book. I first met Adeolu near the end of 2015, while she was leading strategy for a multinational in Turkey. Despite being heavily pregnant with her second child, she had both an unwavering belief in Africa and an infectious enthusiasm that were incredibly inspiring. Obviously, I asked her to join our team, and we worked together for half a decade across a dozen African markets. Adeolu's unique and stylish (dress reference fully intended!) blend of global experience, multicultural exposure, and deeply African roots make her distinctively qualified to share her insights on building successful businesses on the continent.

Afro-Optimism Unleashed is a unique and invaluable guide for African business leaders aspiring to achieve global excellence. Drawing on her extensive experience building successful businesses across the continent, Adeolu offers practical insights and actionable strategies that can help you navigate the challenges and opportunities of the African business landscape. There are very few, if any, such books that are for Africans by an African and that are additionally based on such genuine personal experience – real and practical, not just theory.

Africa is a continent of immense potential, with a diverse range of markets and opportunities. While each of its fifty-four countries has its own unique story, the majority offer favorable conditions for business growth, including reasonable governance and institutions. As Adeolu and I together have observed, reliable and fair judicial systems are essential for creating a stable and predictable business environment.

African talent is abundant, but it often lacks international exposure and adequate funding. *Afro-Optimism Unleashed* offers practical guidance on overcoming these challenges, including strategies for gaining global experience and accessing capital. Adeolu provides an amusing anecdote that reveals African talent's lack of exposure, in which everybody thinks the fish from their country is the best. However, as Adeolu points out, African professionals who have had the opportunity to work in international settings often thrive, demonstrating their ability to operate at the highest standards while maintaining their strong cultural identity.

I've had the privilege of working with many talented African professionals who have gone on to achieve great success in global organizations. Adeolu's ability to identify and nurture such talent is a testament to her expertise on and commitment to African excellence. In fact, one of the elements that makes Adeolu a strong thought leader is the fact that many young Kenyans, Senegalese, Ivorians, Nigerians, Ghanaians, and others who have worked with and for her have gone on to become CEOs, CFOs, and COOs for large multinationals.

The pace of change in Africa is truly remarkable. On every trip I take to cities like Dakar, Casablanca, Abidjan, Accra, Lagos, Kigali, or Nairobi, I witness new factories, roads, restaurants, and other developments springing up. Despite the challenges, Africa is undeniably on the move. The continent's growing middle class is creating a vibrant market for goods and services, fueling further growth and development. Sometimes there are setbacks, and inevitably it's one step back for every three steps forward, but Africa keeps moving.

This perception mismatch is also a secret success lever, as it allows local entrepreneurs and business leaders to build thriving local businesses, then pan-African businesses with very few global competitors, a great basis from which to go global thereafter.

Adeolu skillfully weaves her decades of experience into a straightforward SCALE framework, providing a practical guide for African entrepreneurs. *Strategizing Your Vision* involves defining a clear and compelling purpose for your business that aligns with African realities and can be scaled. *Championing Excellence* emphasizes the importance of finding and developing top African talent to drive innovation and performance. *Accelerating Leadership* concerns tools and strategies for ensuring that you and your leadership team are equipped to navigate the challenges and opportunities of the African business landscape. *Leveraging Governance* highlights the critical role of trust and accountability in building a successful and sustainable business. Finally, *Expanding with Capital* involves accessing the funding needed to scale your business and achieve your goals. By following this framework, African entrepreneurs can unlock the continent's vast potential and create lasting value.

Capturing Adeolu's wisdom and passion and drawing on her extensive experience and insights, this book provides a roadmap for aspiring African leaders to achieve global impact. Its message is not just for African business leaders, however; anyone interested in global development or entrepreneurship will find valuable lessons and inspiration in these pages.

More than just a book, *Afro-Optimism Unleashed* is a call to action. Adeolu challenges African leaders to take pride in their heritage, strive for global relevance, and harness the continent's unique strengths to create lasting change. By following the practical strategies outlined in this book, you can unlock your potential, build a thriving business, and contribute to Africa's bright future.

Coenraad Vrolijk
Chief Executive Officer and Co-founder,
CarbonPool (Switzerland)

Introduction

I have always been ambitious. Growing up as the eldest child in an educated Nigerian family, just a stone's throw away from the campus of one of the largest research universities in the USA, if not the globe, and with one of its top professors as a father, I was never troubled by the silly notion that girls aren't supposed to be ambitious. In fact, it was likely this trait that connected me even further with my father. As a Nigerian, particularly as the firstborn, I was meant to be the best. Long before I ever heard the expression *Naija no dey carry last* (Nigerians never give up), I knew what was expected of me: good grades above sports (and perhaps even church). And good grades meant nothing less than an A. How many times had I heard my dad's story about the time he came home with a mark of 99%, and his own farmer father (who had never even made it to secondary school) asked him, "But where is that 1%?"

So believe me when I say that I know what it means to be ambitious, to be primed from birth to be number one, to have a relentless pursuit of excellence become the cornerstone of your life. It doesn't only come from ego, although you can be allowed a glow of pride at your success; rather, it comes from not knowing any other way and not wanting to let down parents who have sacrificed so much. It also comes from knowing that it is up to you to pay this sacrifice forward and to dream big, not just for yourself, but for the next generation – for whom you must push Africa and Africans to finally realize our potential.

If you're an ambitious African like me, then this book is for you. If you have always pushed yourself to be number one, perhaps even going so far as to achieve that seeming pinnacle of business success – the title of CEO – then welcome. However, while we Africans are known for our ambition, we're also renowned for our resilience. To truly excel on this continent, we must fully leverage both qualities.

Because with all my ambition, as a global Nigerian – a child of the African diaspora, if you will – I've also had to be resilient. Born in the homeland but shifted elsewhere at the age of three, I had to learn to navigate diverse cultures and economies from a very young age, until I found myself eight years and multiple moves later surrounded by cows...and books. But I knew that one day I would return home, and so I proceeded to make building the new Africa my life's mission.

The journey home took me much longer than I could have anticipated, from the skyscrapers of the windy city of Chicago, to the "*Altbau*" (historic buildings) of Munich. A hop, skip, and jump took me to Istanbul (the historic city of Constantinople), before I found myself, a mere seventeen years into my career, on my first business flight to Nairobi. So today, with a quarter-century of experience under my heels – as an international consultant, a global executive, a strategic investor who has poured both passion and capital (a mere half-billion euros' worth!) into the heart of Africa, a CEO who has been tasked with managing one of those investments in one of the most challenging business environments in the world in the midst of one of the most tumultuous times in modern history – my story has been one of bridging worlds and fostering growth. One of connection, rather than of competition. One showcasing the collaborative excellence and spirit of African innovation that I continue to bring to the global stage. I've witnessed firsthand the potential of African markets. I've invested in promising ventures, led successful teams, and survived countless hurdles. My story is one of ambition, perseverance, and resilience, plus a deep-rooted belief in Africa's ability to thrive on the global stage.

But being a CEO sucks. Let's just put that out there. Oh, there's the glamour, the privilege, sometimes the money, and all that's great. But whether you head up a large conglomerate or lead a promising young entity, you're faced with sleepless nights spent pondering why you can't get your business to grow. There's the weight of responsibility for all those families and all those livelihoods that are relying on you for security and sustainability. There's the daunting task of executing a strategy that aligns with your purpose and your vision, while dealing with shareholders who are quickly losing patience and just want to see the promised return on their money. There's the intricate dance of navigating proper corporate governance in a market where that can be seen as a hindrance rather than a strength. So, if that's your experience, I see you. I see you, tirelessly searching for that perfect team member who can share the load. I see you, chasing the ever-elusive capital that seems just out of reach. I see you, trying to transform an organization while avoiding a pivot that may just jeopardize everything that you've built. And I see you, dealing with international investors who think they understand the local context better than you, who live in it every day. I understand these challenges firsthand, and this book is my commitment to you, to accompany you into the uncertainty, into the loneliness, and into the hopelessness of the CEO life, and to steer you along a path of excellence and growth.

I will walk with you to ensure that you not just survive but thrive in the competitive landscape of business in Africa. I will provide you with my insights and experiences, so that you can also learn how to infuse global best practices within your own local insights, creating a sustainable business that stands out to investors. I will guide you through the process of building a team that shares your vision and has the skills to propel your company forward. I will walk you through the very strategies that help my clients attract talent that doesn't just fill a role but propels their company forward. Clients who have worked with me, from CEOs of startups to leaders of legacy institutions, have achieved sustainable business practices, secured funding, and positioned themselves for global competitiveness. Together, we will chart a course toward a future where your African organization is not just a local success story, but a global phenomenon.

Through this book, we will embark on a transformative journey together, one that will take your business from its current state to become a shining testament to African excellence. Leveraging over two decades of firsthand experience advising businesses across Africa, Asia, Europe, and North America, I have developed a clear, actionable roadmap for scaling your African business. My SCALE framework is the culmination of these experiences and insights, breaking down the complex process into manageable steps and ensuring you have the tools and knowledge to achieve your goals. As a global citizen with deep roots in Africa, I bring a unique perspective on the challenges and opportunities facing African entrepreneurs. A cornerstone of my approach is my ability to bridge the gap between Western business practices and African realities to create solutions that can be leveraged globally. We'll start by *Strategizing*, crafting a vision that's not just grand but sustainable. Then, we'll move into *Championing* a team that's not just competent but delivers excellence in its every endeavor. As we *Accelerate*, you'll learn to lead with impact, making decisions that resonate with your team and your market. *Leveraging* governance will be our next step, ensuring that your growth is not just rapid but also sustainable. Finally, we'll tackle *Expansion*, securing the growth capital that will take your business beyond borders and into the annals of African success.

I'm here to support you every step of the way. Let's work together to overcome hurdles and achieve extraordinary results. Together, we'll build a thriving business that leaves a lasting impact. This, indeed, is how we will SCALE your African excellence to the global stage.

Are you ready to embark on this transformative journey together?

PART ONE
BECOMING AN AFRO-OPTIMIST

ONE

Discovering Afro-Optimism

I don't remember when I first stumbled across the term *Afro-optimism*. I just know that when I did, it immediately resonated. I had longed for my continent of birth for as long as I could remember and jumped at every chance to learn and understand more about it. At first my focus was only on my birth country, as I promised my parents and anyone who would listen that I was going back to Nigeria. Even while I dated during college, practically the first thing I told the hapless guys once we started to get to know each other was about this dream I had about going back home. But what did I know? I was taken from my homeland at the tender age of three and had been back only twice.

How I became an Afro-optimist

I grew up in my mini-Africa in the middle of nowhere, USA. Although there were corn fields all around and my friends talked about hunting season just as easily as they talked about which college they would attend, thankfully, I grew up in a college town with a college professor for a dad. That meant that there was a constant parade of students – more specifically, international students – running through my home. They all seemed quite old at the time, but now, having met some of those same students again in adulthood, I realize that they weren't that much older than teenagers. And, although many of them were, of course, Nigerian, some even Yoruba like us, many more of them were not. That was my introduction to the beautiful multiculturalism of our world, backdropped against the sameness of "white America."

Then I got into college myself, where, in a happy happenstance, I was awarded a minority scholarship in addition to the honors scholarship that was expected of me as the ambitious, straight-A child of educated immigrant parents (remember, *Naija no dey carry last!*). This minority scholarship drew me into another world, filled with other kids, most of whom, like me, were also the children of immigrants, many from the Caribbean. They were Black like me, with skin like mine and hair like my own, but from an entirely different culture, upbringing, and way of thinking. And so my worldview evolved, expanding to include my new Black

American and Caribbean friends with their parties, the Asian kids from the one Asian fraternity on campus, and the Japanese kids I met while studying abroad in Japan, before I finally found my way back to the infamous African Students Club, where we Africans all gathered. Here I met my very first Eritrean; discovered how tall the Sudanese are; observed how much the boys fawned over the Ethiopian women. We were our very own melting pot, and I loved it.

I had to leave this multicultural bubble at some point, but by then it was too late – I had been bitten even harder by the Africa bug. So, when I told the senior executive at the final interview for my first consulting job that I would be opening a subsidiary in Nigeria, I meant it with every fiber of my being. Then came the challenge: I was convinced that the only way to make that happen was to get out of the USA. It's tough to open a Nigerian office stuck in another country, and as we didn't yet have any locations in Africa at all, where could I go from here? I started raising my hand for any and every international opportunity, only to have my application rejected first in Mexico and then in Brazil. Turning my eyes to Europe, I then tried for roles in both London and Zurich and failed to win either of them. However, a project with European colleagues finally had them knocking on my door for a spot in Paris, which I was considering, until Munich popped up with an unexpected offer. So, after a couple of chats on the phone, a quick look-see trip to the office, some painless negotiations, and one seamless immigration process, I was on a business-class flight to Germany, kicking off the first step of my nine-year journey – perhaps, more accurately, my thirty-seven-year journey – back to Africa. And a new Afro-optimist was born.

Why West is *not* (always) best

You may be wondering, *Why Africa?* I'd somehow "escaped," had the privilege of Western schooling, and even managed to get a nice gig in nice, safe, lovely Munich, where expats go to die. Why would I leave all that to come back to a continent filled with hardship and poverty?

I still clearly recall the face of my German head of human resources (HR) when I told him that I would be taking only twelve weeks of parental leave after the birth of my first child. He was too polite, or perhaps liked me too much, to put into words the thoughts running through his head. However, seven-and-a-half years of life in Germany, numerous books about German culture, and endless questions posed to my German colleagues meant I was well aware of the attitudes many Germans still had about the role of women, spectacularly encapsulated by the concept of *Kinder, Küche, Kirche*, or *kids, kitchen, church*. For a country with such a powerful female role model at the top, Angela Merkel (this was back in 2013), it was sometimes depressing for me to see how backward the German ideas of a woman's role in the workplace could be, and how many limitations were placed on women in German society. I never understood how such well-educated and traveled people – it seemed like almost everyone I worked with had a doctorate, including the aforementioned Angela Merkel – couldn't understand how a system that allowed, and actually encouraged, women to remain home for three years after each birth may not be amenable to supporting a woman's ascent up the career ladder if she so choose.

However, having grown up in the USA, which unfortunately went too far in the other direction, with no mandatory parental leave and most new mothers being expected to take off only three months, I was quite certain that I could make this work. Thankfully, I had the fortune of working with a great boss who not only pushed me to be the best I could be, but who, although childless himself, understood the importance of family. It was our strong communication and my laying out a plan to continue to push his grand plans for the organization that gave me the leeway and flexibility to focus on my baby for those first twelve weeks, then find the best hybrid working solution for us – and this all long before the days of a global pandemic that would make hybrid and even remote working the norm. However, I was a former consultant and a disciplined and ambitious Nigerian, and I knew that I could make it work.

So I would jump up early in the morning, nurse the baby before heading out for my morning run, carefully shower and dress downstairs in our duplex apartment, so that I wouldn't wake the baby, who was sound asleep again upstairs, and rush out the door to make it into the office by 7am. Around 10am, I would check, double-check, and sometimes triple-check that I had locked both doors to my office, pull out my breast pump, and spend about thirty minutes emptying both breasts into those precious milk bags. Then I would rush home around midday, so that my husband, then partner, could rush out the door to his own business selling up-market window dressings. I would put the baby down for a nap around 3pm, and our weekly cleaner, who had graduated to daily cleaner and nanny with the advent of the baby, would arrive around 4pm after her full-time job, to give me a couple of hours of peace to take a few meetings without baby in tow. Bath and bedtime by 7pm allowed me another couple of hours, and then I was up the next morning at 5am to do the same.

It was exhausting for both of us, and there were moments when my partner would hurl his phone at the wall in exasperation, declaring that he couldn't take this pace another day. Thankfully, fourteen months into this nerve-racking schedule, we moved to Turkey, where we could easily afford a full-time, live-in nanny, giving us the luxury of even managing a second child. And then finally – finally – we moved back to Africa, to Kenya, to be specific, where we could hire an entire support system to help us manage work and family, with a housekeeper, a nanny, a driver, and even a gardener to take care of the grounds surrounding our two-floor, 400-square-meter, modern country home. And, for the first time since I had become a parent, I could exhale and really start climbing even further up that corporate ladder.

So when, during a recent one-month visit to the USA, people simply assumed that I would be coming back, the idea screamed to me, *No*. *No*, I would not fall into the trap of the standard dual-income family setup in the West, where you need both salaries to even afford some semblance of sanity as a working parent, but then are driven to insanity by the constant daily treadmill of "work-life balance." *No*, I would not go back to a society that would not value my two half-Nigerian, half-Turkish boys with four passports between them as much as they valued their own children. *No*, I would not go back to a society where I couldn't claim my heritage quite as loudly as I could on my own continent. With my bright colors, my colorful prints, my Afro-hair. *No*, the West is *not* always best, and every additional day I remain on my continent helps me to see that even more clearly.

Identifying your inner Afro-optimist

OK, so escaping to the West is perhaps not the best, but living here isn't easy either. How do we go about finding optimism amid difficult situations? If you're of a certain age and grew up in the USA, you couldn't have gone without seeing *Coming to America* at least once. This movie perhaps transformed Eddie Murphy from a lowly comedian to a movie star, similar to how *Bad Boys* catapulted Will Smith and *Bridesmaids* transformed Melissa McCarthy. A quite popular movie in the 1990s, *Coming to America* always made my eyes roll, as it chronicled the tale of some made-up prince from a made-up country in Africa with an even more ridiculous made-up accent! It seemed really the epitome of what Black Americans thought or hoped Africa was like. However, as much as I winced every time I watched the movie, one thing I had to admit was that all the fake opulence and privilege that the prince and his entourage showcased was much better than the commercials that continually rolled during that same time, showing "starving Ethiopian kids" who just needed $1 from America to save them. Welcome to my life as an African in the USA in the 1990s. Yet, throughout all the misconceptions I saw on television about the continent of my birth, all the jokes my "friends" made about Africans living in trees, despite the way I knew Blacks were treated in the USA, I never lost my pride as an African, and more specifically, as a Nigerian. While I stumbled across the term "Afro-optimism" much, much later, I knew from the very first day my family "came to America" that there would also be a "day of return" for me, when I would finally find myself back on the soil where I belonged.

So, what exactly is Afro-optimism? The concept emerged in the late 2010s to emphasize the positivity, progress, and celebration of our African identity and our achievements. It stands in contrast to the usual cynicism and negative bias that often leads individuals of African descent to have a pessimistic outlook on our future. Afro-optimism focuses on highlighting Africa's modernity, inspiring action, and showcasing our continent's potential for leadership and innovation. It aims to counter negative stereotypes and perceptions about Africa by promoting a more positive and empowering narrative that recognizes our continent's rich history, resources, and contributions to global development.

Afro-optimism isn't just a buzzword; it's a mindset, a movement, a mandate. It's about flipping the script on Africa's story, swapping tales of despair for dreams of dominance. We're not just shaking off the shackles of the past; we're forging a future where Africa leads, not follows. We're highlighting Africa's modernity, progress, and unique culture, showcasing the continent's advancements in various sectors like science, technology, the arts, and peacebuilding. Afro-optimism means celebrating our uniqueness, our resilience, our innovation. It's about showcasing our tech hubs, our booming creative industries, and our groundbreaking research. It's about telling the world that Africa is not a monolith of poverty, but a diverse continent brimming with potential.

But it's more than just talk. Afro-optimism is about action. It's about backing and investing in our own people and supporting our own businesses. It's about demanding excellence, holding leaders accountable, and fostering a culture of innovation by celebrating outstanding achievements and leadership in Africa, encouraging others to act by serving humanity and making a positive impact on society. Most importantly, Afro-optimism is about believing in ourselves. It's about knowing that we have what it takes to compete on the global stage and win. It's about refusing to be defined by stereotypes and limitations. It's about daring to dream big and working tirelessly to make those dreams a reality, celebrating "Africanness," or African solutions, uniqueness, and progress.

Afro-optimism isn't just a feel-good slogan, though; it's the rocket fuel igniting Africa's entrepreneurial spirit. By celebrating our successes, we inspire a new generation of go-getters. By believing in our potential, we create a magnetic force that draws investment and talent. By showcasing our innovation, we challenge stereotypes and build a platform for our entrepreneurs to shine. Afro-optimism is even more than a mindset; it's a movement that's connecting the continent and its diaspora, creating a powerful ecosystem for growth.

Now, while Afro-optimism emphasizes positivity, progress, and the celebration of African identity and achievements, it also acknowledges our continent's challenges and complexities. Afro-optimism does not ignore the negative aspects of Africa's reality. It simply aims to provide a more balanced and empowering narrative that recognizes both the challenges and the potential for progress while inspiring action and celebrating achievements. In short, Afro-optimism embraces the complexities of the African experience.

While I'm not a psychologist, it's obvious to me how my own brand of Afro-optimism has informed my outlook in life. I consider myself a realistic optimist, and the African twist has resulted in maintaining a consistently positive outlook on Africa's future and our own massive potential for success. It focuses my outlook on our continent's progress, our innovation, and our achievements, and really sets the frame for my sense of hope and optimism even with, and despite, much evidence to the contrary. My Afro-optimism, combined with my knowledge of the West, pushes me to confront negative stereotypes, tackle challenges head-on, and continue working toward building a better future, if not for myself, then for the two little global Africans following in my footsteps. When people wonder where my self-assurance comes from, I know that it's more than the result of the experiences I had before I reached my forties, or even as I now approach my fifties; it's also a complete belief in my capabilities and potential for growth and development, especially as an African.

So how do you go about finding optimism amid your own situation? You tap into your own inner Afro-optimist and leverage it as a force for change. Afro-optimists are the fuel that will propel Africa forward, and it's up to each of us to contribute to this movement.

Overcoming impostor syndrome

While optimism and resilience are key to our success, it's essential to acknowledge the challenges that come with this journey. Despite the remarkable achievements of African leaders and entrepreneurs, many of us still grapple with feelings of inadequacy. This phenomenon, often referred to as *impostor syndrome*, is particularly prevalent in a context marked by unique pressures and expectations. Impostor syndrome is a condition broadly summarized as a fear you will be found out to not be as good as others think you are.

The relief is that you're not alone. A recent study (Nicols, 2021) found the following:

- 65% of professionals surveyed recognized the symptoms of impostor syndrome, but did not know the term.

- 53% of professional women between twenty-five and thirty-four reported that they currently experienced impostor syndrome, and 75% of executive women reported having experienced it in the past.

- However, less than 5% of employers are doing anything to address this issue with their staff.

The term *impostor phenomenon* was coined after a 1978 study that looked at the experiences of high-achieving women (Clance and Imes, 1978). Today, experts estimate that approximately three in five individuals have experienced feelings of impostor syndrome. So, you can see that impostor syndrome is rather common, impacts both men and women, and many (including employers themselves) still feel it is taboo to discuss it.

Sometimes people ask me whether I have ever encountered impostor syndrome myself. Hmmm...have I ever felt that maybe I'm not good enough? That I don't belong? That soon, somebody, somewhere, will catch me out? I must think long and hard when I encounter that question, because decades of building up my expertise and collecting achievements have told me what I need to know. And, as a mathematician who tends more to the analytical side, I simply allow the facts to speak for themselves.

But the reality is that I have often been the only one in the room. Whether it was the only woman, the only person of color, the only African, the only person with an American accent, the youngest, now the oldest... I'm used to being different – too many times, obviously different. So how do I manage? I can't change who I am; all I can do is to lean into that difference and make sure that my difference makes me memorable. My difference often allows me to transform "the only" into "the expert."

Here are five ways you can channel your inner Afro-optimist and leverage your unique background and experiences as strengths, rather than sources of insecurity:

1. **Identify and appreciate your unique talents:** Do you know that feeling when you're in your zone, completely absorbed in what you're doing? That's your inner Afro-optimist shining through. It's helpful to recognize the magic within you, the stuff that sets you apart. Maybe it's how you can whip up a killer presentation at the last minute, or the way you effortlessly connect with people from all walks of life. Trust me, we all have these superpowers; it's just about discovering them.

2. **Develop your talents further:** You've got the spark; now it's time to fan the flames. Don't just sit on your talent; nurture it, feed it, watch it grow. Whether it's attending coding bootcamps or design workshops or mastering the art of storytelling, it's important to level up your game. Some think of me as a queen who slays dragons. However, I didn't just wake up breathing fire. I practiced. A lot.

3. **Craft your personal brand:** Your personal brand is your crown jewel. It's how the world sees you, and it's time to make it sparkle. Don't be afraid to shout about your awesomeness. Let the world know what you're bringing to the table. Are you a problem-solving wizard, a creative genius, or a people person? Own it. Remember, your brand isn't just about looking good; it's about making a statement about your impact.

4. **Communicate your achievements:** Don't be shy about tooting your own horn. Your achievements are your battle scars, your proof of greatness. Numbers don't lie, but stories ignite. Share your wins, big or small. Talk about that time you turned a challenge into a triumph, or how your unique perspective rocked the boat (in a good way). Let your light shine!

5. **Embrace a growth mindset:** Adopt an attitude that encourages continuous learning and improvement. Stay curious, embrace challenges, and view setbacks as opportunities for growth. Keep your eyes peeled for what's next, and don't be shy about asking for feedback. Remember, every "no" is one step closer to a "yes." By recognizing, developing, and effectively communicating your strengths, you can turn potential insecurities into powerful assets that propel your career forward. Your story is still being written, so make it a bestseller.

When you're the only African in the room, remember that can also make you the smartest person in the room...when it comes to Africa. So feel free to pepper your narrative highlighting other successful African professionals and showcasing your own successes. Embrace and show off how our unique experiences and insights can lead to fresh and innovative business solutions that cater to the specific needs of the African market. And don't forget to collaborate. Black

Americans tend to understand the power of acknowledging and lifting up their brothers and sisters in the room; we, as Africans, need to do the same when it comes to collaborating with other professionals, clients, and stakeholders in the African business community. By implementing these strategies, you can effectively recognize and acknowledge your own achievements and expertise in the African business context, positioning yourself as a valuable and respected professional within the region.

Now, a side note for women leaders: African women leaders navigate a unique labyrinth of challenges, with impostor syndrome being a particularly formidable foe. The pressure to fit into molds that often don't exist for us is a constant balancing act – don't be too soft, don't be too tough. Add to that the scarcity of female role models, and it's like climbing a mountain blindfolded. Our cultures, while rich in tradition, can also be restrictive, making it even harder to own our power. But let's be clear: we're not victims. We're warriors. By breaking down barriers, supporting each other, and demanding a seat at the table, we can not only overcome these obstacles but also redefine leadership on the African continent.

Finally, while individual empowerment is crucial, the power of collective action cannot be overstated. By fostering a sense of collaboration among African professionals, we can create a more supportive and empowering environment. This means building strong networks, mentoring and sponsoring the next generation, and advocating for policies that support African talent. Imagine a world where African professionals are not just individuals overcoming challenges, but a united force driving positive change. By sharing knowledge, resources, and experiences, we can amplify our impact and create a more equitable future. Let's harness the power of collective action to build a stronger, more resilient African professional community.

Are you ready to unleash the Afro-optimist within? It's time to rewrite your story, own your power, and create a legacy that inspires generations. You can transform potential into reality, doubt into determination, and challenges into triumphs. Join the movement of African excellence. The world is waiting. Are you ready to make your mark?

Embracing your awesomeness

When I decided to make the move from consulting to corporate, it shouldn't have been a huge surprise that I ended up in the global HR department of one of my clients – my largest one in fact, the one I, myself, had landed – given that these were people who had worked with me already. Perhaps a year after I joined this rather international group, led by a Swiss man, we got a new head of compensation and benefits, an American. Given my connection with the USA, I tend to get along quite easily with Americans, and it was no different in this case. One day as we were chatting, he shook his head in disbelief at something I'd just said and exclaimed, "Adeolu, you're such a dichotomy. You've managed to get a mix of everything...an American accent, a German mind, and a Nigerian heart." That summed it up so well that I never forgot that phrase.

While I've leaned into and maintained who I am as a person, through my status as a "third-culture kid" and the various moves I've made over my still-short life, I've also been very open to absorbing the best of each culture while remaining very much me. A colleague looked at my company website one day and asked it if I had built it myself. Given this colleague's light, but constant, teasing over my lack of creativity when it came to graphics, I braced for his response but proudly said yes. He went on to say that he did love the website and was quite impressed, but that he could tell as he was going through it that it had my voice – and this was someone who had known me less than three months!

And that is how I embrace my own awesomeness. I know who I am, what I represent, how I present myself, the way I speak...these are all building blocks for my personal brand as "Adeolu the Afro-optimist." Much of this was not intentional; it just stemmed from my own purpose for my life, my lifelong pride as a global Nigerian, and my confidence, cemented now in my late forties, of who I am as a person. As I told an interviewer during my very first podcast appearance, "Take me as I am."

That's what we all need to do: remember that there's only one of each of us. So what's your unique life story, and how can you leverage that as a child or friend of Africa? Many times, I've regretted that my dad didn't send me back to Nigeria for high school as he had planned, or that I can't speak my own mother tongue as fluently as a native, or even that we didn't move to France, rather than an anglophone country, so that I could at least speak French (rather than German, Spanish, etc.). But then I shrug my shoulders and remember that it's my own life experiences that have made me who I am today. I certainly can't change them; I can only use them.

The wonderful thing is, when you know who you are, and, more critically, are comfortable with it, you find your own unique brand of inspiration and leadership that will draw the right people – your people – to you. My Afro-optimism can be seen not just in my pride in my dark skin and kinky hair, but in the way that I dress myself. This has shifted as I've moved from country to country. What presented itself in bright and vibrant colors when I lived in the West quickly transformed into my own brand of "Afro-corporate" dress when we moved to Nairobi. Whether it's my Ankara jacket top, my Kente pencil dress, my crafted Kenyan jewelry, or my Maasai slippers on more casual days, I almost always have something African on me. Given that we were on the continent, I didn't realize that people actually took note of my style choices during my travels until I became CEO in my home country for one of the companies that I had helped acquire, and colleagues routinely mentioned how they'd always admired my boldness when they encountered me during my acquisition trips, with one Afro-print style or another.

I'm quite sure there are enough folks to whom my Afro-pride doesn't appeal. Not professional. Too in-your-face. Trying too hard. Not conservative enough. Too simple. Too informal. I can imagine some or all this running through some people's heads. But once I understood that I didn't need to be liked by everyone, I also realized that I just didn't care. Take me as I am.

Final thoughts

Your journey is unique, your potential limitless. It's time to embrace your authentic self, celebrate your African heritage, and redefine success on your own terms. Together, we can build an awesome movement of confident, empowered individuals who are reimagining what it means to be African in the global arena. Let's create a future where our voices are heard, our contributions celebrated, and our dreams realized. Are you ready to become an Afro-optimist?

TWO
Building A Global Mindset

As I said earlier, becoming an Afro-optimist doesn't make you blind to the rest of the world. In fact, our Afro-optimism must and should be couched in the context of what is going on globally, particularly if we don't want to be left behind or, worse, miss the next big thing. Even in the imaginary nation of the Black Panther's Wakanda, which many see as a potential fulfillment of our African aspirations, residents are keenly aware of the outside world, even as they close themselves off from it. For generations, Wakanda cloaks itself in secrecy, its advanced society fueled by the mythical Vibranium. Yet, beneath the surface of self-sufficiency hums a hidden reliance on the global market. Vibranium's unmatched properties may have propelled Wakanda forward, but its true value hinges on the world's insatiable hunger for technological leaps.

Without that external pressure, Wakanda's innovations might have remained stagnant, curiosities within a closed system.

This paradox, this dance between isolation and integration, lies at the heart of Afro-optimism. Africa, a continent brimming with potential, must harness its own resources and cultivate self-reliance. But to truly thrive, we need to understand the ever-shifting currents of the global economy. Wakanda's story serves as a potent reminder: even the most self-sufficient nation dances to a global tune. So let's break down the global playbook from an African perspective.

Principle 1: Embrace the digital revolution

The digital revolution is sweeping across the globe, and Africa is no exception. From bustling markets going digital to classrooms without walls, our continent is rewriting the rules of business. This isn't just a trend; it's a revolution. So how do you ride this wave?

- **Become an e-commerce powerhouse:** Forget the stuffy old stores. The future of shopping is in your hands (or rather, your smartphone). Build a brand that people crave and deliver it right to their doorstep. Africa may be a big place, but with e-commerce, your market can be even bigger.

- **Develop mobile magic:** Mobile is king in Africa. People live on their phones. Create apps that connect, educate and solve problems. Whether you're empowering farmers with smart agricultural tools or bringing education to remote villages, the possibilities are endless.

- **Unlock the power of data:** Data is your secret weapon. It's the crystal ball that reveals your customers' desires. Use data to create products people love, target your marketing like a pro, and stay ahead of the curve.

This is no longer our grandfather's economy. Move fast, break things (gently), and partner up. Collaborate with tech wizards, learn from failures, and most importantly, have fun. By becoming a key player in Africa's digital transformation, you'll not only propel your business forward but also contribute to shaping a more technologically advanced future for the continent.

Principle 2: Build a pan-African powerhouse

Africa is a continent of fifty-four nations, each with its own unique culture and resources. But imagine a united front of African businesses, a force to be reckoned with on the global stage. This is the vision behind the African Continental Free Trade Area (AfCFTA). Officially launched on January 1, 2021, following its signing in March 2018, AfCFTA aims to create a single market for goods and services across these same fifty-four countries, connecting approximately 1.3 billion people with a combined GDP of about $3.4 trillion, and potentially lifting 50 million people out of extreme poverty (World Bank Group, 2022).

So how do you make this vision a reality?

- **Forge powerful partnerships:** Networking isn't just about shaking hands; it's about building bridges. Connect with fellow entrepreneurs across the continent. Share knowledge, resources, and customers. After all, we're stronger together.

- **Create products for the continent:** Africa is diverse, but our challenges and aspirations often unite us. Develop solutions that resonate with people from Cape Town to Cairo. From agriculture to tech, there's a massive market waiting to be conquered.

- **Be a changemaker:** Talk is cheap, but action speaks volumes. Get involved in shaping the policies that will make AfCFTA a success by lobbying to ensure that any agreements are as generous as possible and supporting your government in building broad public support. Your voice matters. Let's create an environment where African businesses can thrive.

By embracing AfCFTA, we can contribute to a more integrated African market, driving collaboration and unlocking immense economic potential. Remember, a rising tide lifts all boats – when African businesses thrive together, the entire continent benefits.

Principle 3: Leave a legacy that lasts

Money isn't everything. Sure, it's nice, but leaving a positive mark on the world is priceless. Likewise, success in Africa isn't just about financial gain; it's about building a sustainable legacy for future generations. Imagine a future where businesses operate with environmental responsibility, empower their communities, and prioritize ethical practices. This is the essence of a sustainable business model, and it's becoming increasingly important for African entrepreneurs. So how can you integrate sustainability into your business?

- **Do the right thing:** Transparency, ethics, and fairness are the cornerstones of a lasting business. Play fair, treat your employees right, and build trust. Your reputation is everything.

- **Empower your community:** Success is sweeter when shared. Invest in the people surrounding you. Create jobs, support education, and give back. Your community is your biggest asset.

- **Be a planet protector:** Our continent is blessed with natural beauty. Let's keep it that way. From solar panels to recycled packaging, make your business eco-friendly. It's good for the planet, and it's good for business.

Be more than just a business owner; be a change leader. By fusing innovation, impact, and integrity, you're not just building a company; you're shaping Africa's future. Let's redefine success as being about more than the bottom line. It's about creating a legacy that uplifts communities and preserves our planet. Join the movement of African entrepreneurs who are proving that "Made in Africa" equals business for good. Are you ready to make your mark?

The sun dips below the Vibranium-rich mountains of mythical Wakanda, casting a golden glow across a nation unlike any other. Here, amid fields of unyielding optimism and technological marvels, a powerful truth emerges: isolation may breed progress, but true prosperity flourishes when we understand the world beyond our borders.

Developing a global vision and strategy

My purpose statement is to build the new Africa, and that's the legacy I want to leave so that my two boys (as of this writing, ages eleven and nine) grow up as proud global Africans. That's it. Nice and simple. But translating that purpose into my global vision, and then into strategies for my business, is not so simple. What does it mean to be a "global African"? What is the "new Africa" that will facilitate that? Is the timeframe for what I call "Vision 2033" – about a decade, since we launched in 2023 – long enough? What does being a global African say about how and where I bring up the boys themselves? What kind of leader do I need to be, and what kind of people do I need to work with to accomplish all this? I certainly can't do it alone.

These questions and more are what run through my mind as I think about the future and consider my past. As I consider my upbringing in a large college town in the USA, contemplate what I learned from the precise Germans during my almost decade in Munich, and even incorporate tidbits of Asia, via Japan and Turkey, into my pan-African view of the continent, I know this experience informs my view of what it is to be a "global Nigerian," a label I wear with pride. I remember the first time I heard Chimamanda Ngozi Adichie's 2009 speech about the danger of a single story, when she said, "Stories matter. Many stories matter...when we reject the single story, when we realize that there is never a single story about any place, we regain a kind of paradise."

So I must tap into my own story and leverage the stories of the many others I encounter in considering what this "new Africa" can look like. I tap into my story as a Nigerian diasporan. I tap into my colleague's story as a Nigerian schooled in the East. I tap into my business partner's story as a white South African woman. I tap into my client's story as a Ugandan living in Nairobi. I tap into another business partner's story as an Egyptian who worked for an international company all his career. I even tap into the story of yet another business partner who is a white Brit living in the UK, yet has focused his entire career on the African continent. Continuously tapping into all these stories, into all these various experiences, causes me to adjust and shift my view of what this "new Africa" will look like, because the newness must build on the old. And I leverage the trust given to me by people telling me their stories into a vision of trusted partners building the new Africa together.

And how do we build the "new Africa"? Might it take less time doing it together vs. running on our own? Best practice. Collaboration. Networking. These are the approaches that jump out at me as I ponder my global vision. The best thing about such approaches is their accessibility across cultures. As combative as we humans are, as prone to violence and automatic "othering" of people we deem outsiders, our glorious benefit is that we strive for connection. And business strategies that tap into that need for connection can be transcendent. My willingness to share with you opens you up to sharing with me and to collaborating, opening your network, being willing to incorporate best practices that may come from "outsiders."

While living in Nairobi, I was surrounded by several young colleagues in their twenties, none of whom had experienced life outside the borders of Kenya. They rightfully took immense pride in their culture, loudly proclaiming why such and such a thing was the best in the world, including the ubiquitous tilapia fish which seemed to be ever-present at any restaurant. Finally, one day, I asked these colleagues – again, none of whom had crossed the Kenyan border – how they knew that tilapia was the best fish in the world? Had they tried any others? I listened in bemusement as they tried to convince me that there was no need to try any other fish, given that they had already had the best. "Fine," I told them. "How about this. Let me take you to a seafood restaurant, my treat." They were initially reluctant, but finally accepted the challenge. So, one night, we all ended up at Seven Seafood & Grill, one of the best seafood restaurants in Nairobi. I dragged along my Turkish husband because, truth be told, I don't even like fish, but I couldn't allow this distaste to stop me from providing my colleagues a life lesson. So my husband rose to the challenge of being a teacher and ordered various dishes from the menu, including several types of fish, shellfish, even octopus, while my colleagues sat and shook their heads in disgust. The plates arrived at our table, and each colleague, not willing to be outdone by the other, nervously tried the proffered delicacies. One of the youngest at first refused to try the octopus, but, egged on by his colleagues, he finally took a leap of faith and popped one portion into his mouth. I still recall his expression as he chewed. And popped in another portion. Then – victory – he turned to my husband and asked him if we could possibly order more octopus!

I carry this experience around with me as a reminder of what can happen when we extend from our own area of expertise (not seafood!) to tap into our network (in this case, I didn't have to look that far) and collaborate on building capacity (for seafood), leveraging the best practice we could find (a top seafood restaurant). That's the power we achieve when we transcend borders to redefine our Africanness.

Leveraging global insights for local impact

So, understanding the power of border-crossing for collaboration, I love having a squad of super-smart business besties scattered across the globe, and I love to tell the story of my early days, back when IBM's Lotus Sametime was still a thing. Perhaps the reason I love WhatsApp so much is that it reminds me of those days, when I, based in Chicago, could chat with a colleague in New York, Paris, or Tokyo as easily as I could walk around the corner to knock on the door of my work bestie. I was working then as a founding member of my company's global consulting team, and Sametime became a necessary tool for our success. It also became the start of my global squad-building. I had the European Investment Bank (EIB), the European Union's investment bank and the largest multilateral financial institution in the world, as a client. One of my team members was based in Paris. As we worked daily on that client, as tends to happen, personal details and life happenings started to get sprinkled into the work conversation. Over the months and years, I read his chats about meeting the girl of his dreams and all the adventures and misfortunes that befell the relationship. Then one day, it happened: he asked the woman to marry him. I rejoiced with him just as mightily as the "real" colleagues in his own office. But what I hadn't expected, never having actually met this colleague in person, or even seen what he looked like (these were the days before selfies and video chats ever crossed people's minds) was that he would actually invite me to his wedding. This invite, even as I think on it now, serves as an unforgettable testament to the bonds we can build with others across the world, made even easier today with tools such as Instagram, LinkedIn, and, of course, WhatsApp.

In our interconnected world, the businesses that thrive are those that can seamlessly navigate global markets while maintaining a deep understanding of local nuances. Leveraging global insights is no longer a luxury; it's a necessity. Let's explore how to turn these far-flung friends into a winning formula.

Cultivating a global mindset

Remember when physically traveling for business meetings seemed like the only option? Thanks to COVID, the world has shrunk (virtually, at least) and opened a treasure chest of opportunities for your business. To effectively leverage global insights, it's essential to cultivate a global mindset, which you can now maintain without even leaving your office. This involves developing a broad perspective, embracing diversity, and being open to new ideas and experiences. By immersing yourself in unfamiliar cultures and business environments, you'll gain a deeper appreciation for the complexities of the global marketplace.

A strong network is the cornerstone of global success. Invest time in building relationships with professionals from different countries and industries. Attend industry conferences, participate in online forums, and leverage social media platforms to connect with potential partners and collaborators. Focus on building authentic relationships based on mutual respect and shared goals. Spark conversations on video calls – a tool we've all become experts in, thanks to COVID – and pick people's brains. They'll spill the 'chai' on best practices in their regions, from what customers are digging to what the competition's up to.

Harnessing technology for collaboration

Technology has revolutionized the way we connect and collaborate with people around the world. Online collaboration tools have become second nature to many of us post-COVID. These tools let us connect with our networks in real time, no matter where they are in the world. From video conferencing and project management software to social media and virtual collaboration spaces, technology can be a powerful enabler of global partnerships – instant innovation, delivered straight to our screens.

Technology is also your secret weapon for glocal market research. To make informed business decisions, it's essential to have a deep understanding of global market trends and consumer behavior. Invest in comprehensive market research to identify opportunities and challenges in different regions. By analyzing data and insights from various sources, you can develop effective strategies to penetrate new markets.

Adapting to local contexts

Glocalization isn't about copying the coolest trends from across the globe. It's about understanding your local market like the back of your hand. While global trends provide valuable insights, it's crucial to adapt your approach to meet the specific needs of local markets. Conduct thorough market research to understand cultural nuances, consumer preferences, and competitive landscapes. By combining global best practices with local knowledge, you can create tailored glocal solutions that resonate with your target audience. Are you revamping your marketing for a new market? Don't just translate your existing campaign; adapt it to local tastes! Think about language localization, cultural references, and communication channels that your new audience frequents.

Here's where the fun part begins: building a glocal team. You'll need a diverse crew with a mix of backgrounds and cultural understanding. Why? Because when it comes to adapting global best practices to your local market, a broader perspective is your best friend. Plus, that team member sitting in Nairobi can be the cultural compass guiding you through regulations and keeping your brand sensitive to the local vibe.

Measuring impact locally

Remember, success is local too. To assess the effectiveness of your global strategy, don't just track global metrics. Develop key performance indicators (KPIs) specific to your local market. These could include customer satisfaction in your region, market share growth within your city, or brand awareness among your local audience. By monitoring local KPIs, you can identify areas for improvement, optimize resource allocation, and measure the overall impact of your global initiatives.

Glocalization isn't a fad; it's the future. It's about building a business that thrives on a global scale, while remaining deeply rooted in its local community. It's about collaborating with awesome people across the world to create a sustainable future. So, get out there (virtually, of course), start building your glocal network, and watch your business blossom on the world stage!

Building a strong online presence and brand

People tend to do business with people they know, like and trust, so if you want to collaborate with awesome people across the world, they need to think of you as an awesome person as well. Therefore, in today's interconnected world, having a strong personal brand is essential for standing out. It's more than just a name or logo; it's a promise to your audience. What unites prominent business personalities like Mo Ibrahim of Celtel, Richard Branson of the Virgin Group, Sheryl Sandberg formerly of Facebook, the late Steve Jobs of Apple, Tony Elumelu of Heirs Holdings, and Oprah Winfrey? In each case, the founder's personal brand and entrepreneurial story are closely intertwined with the success of the company they created.

Let's take Richard Branson as an example; he is a masterclass in building a successful business image. Branson's personal brand isn't just about Virgin companies. He's cultivated an image as a disruptive entrepreneur, an adventurer, and a guy who challenges the status quo. This resonates with people who value innovation, fun, and a bit of daring. The Virgin brand itself might not necessarily scream innovation compared to competitors. But Branson's association with it adds a layer of excitement and a human touch. People are more likely to trust Virgin because they feel they know the kind of person behind it. And Branson isn't afraid to put himself out there. His adventures, like his hot air balloon trips or his attempts to break speed records, get media attention and keep Virgin top of mind. Additionally, Branson comes across as approachable and enthusiastic, even when he talks about his failures, and he seems to genuinely enjoy what he does. This makes people trust him – and Virgin by association. Branson has authored books and actively uses social media to share his stories and ideas. This allows him to shape how people perceive him and Virgin, emphasizing the aspects he wants them to focus on. By creating an emotional connection with his audience, Branson's personal brand makes Virgin more than just a company; it makes it a brand with a personality that people can connect with. This is the power of a well-crafted personal brand.

Oprah Winfrey's journey is another textbook case of how a powerful personal brand can propel someone to extraordinary heights. Oprah didn't try to be another generic talk show host. She brought her own unique perspective, focusing on in-depth conversations, emotional connection, and empowering guests to share their stories. This authenticity and warmth set her apart in a crowded media landscape. She also wasn't shy about putting herself out there. Her engaging interviews with celebrities and everyday people, coupled with her willingness to tackle tough topics, turned her into a household name. Her brand transcended *The Oprah Winfrey Show*, becoming synonymous with empowerment and self-improvement. Additionally, Oprah's vulnerability in sharing her own struggles with poverty, abuse, and weight loss resonated deeply with viewers. She wasn't afraid to show her humanity, which fostered genuine trust and connection with her audience. People believed she understood their problems because she had faced her own. Oprah wasn't just the host of her show; she was the curator of her brand. She carefully chose the topics and guests for her show, ensuring they aligned with her message of empowerment and personal growth. This allowed her to shape the conversation and reinforce the core values of her brand. At the heart of Oprah's brand is connection. She created a space where people felt heard, understood, and uplifted. Her empathy and genuine interest in her guests, along with her willingness to open up about her own life, fostered a powerful emotional bond with her viewers. This connection made her brand so much more than just a media empire; it made it a trusted guide for millions.

Tony Elumelu exemplifies the power of African entrepreneurship. His unwavering commitment to African entrepreneurs, coupled with his philanthropic initiatives, has solidified his reputation as a visionary leader. By aligning his personal brand with his business ventures, Elumelu has created a powerful and influential image. His story of rising from the bottom ranks of the banking industry to acquiring those same banks, including United Bank for Africa in 2005, inspires and empowers an entire generation of African entrepreneurs. His pan-African focus, which demonstrates his deep commitment to the continent's development, is a key element of his success. Additionally, he intentionally puts himself out there as a role model for aspiring business owners while simultaneously giving back to the community and fostering social impact. Finally, his reach on social media builds trust through genuine engagement with his audience.

How do you become as well-known, at least in your own space, as Richard Branson, Oprah Winfrey, and Tony Elumelu? First, forget about mimicking any of them. You are your brand's secret weapon. Embrace the aphorism "Be yourself; everyone else is already taken." Find your brand's voice. Are you the innovator? The trusted adviser? The friendly face? Let your core values shine through every social media post and online channel.

Authenticity is key. Share your brand story, showcase the humans behind the magic, and engage with your audience in real conversations. Spark discussions, answer questions, and build a community around your brand. Testimonials and case studies are gold, showcasing the positive impact you have on real people.

Become a thought leader. Share valuable insights, educate your audience, and empower them with insightful blog posts, videos, and webinars. Raise your hand; representation matters. Speak at panels, join discussions, and position yourself as the trusted resource you are. Go beyond likes and shares. Offer valuable free resources like e-books, white papers, or webinars. Demonstrate your expertise and build trust by providing value without expecting anything in return.

Stories are your superpower. Weave captivating narratives into your social media. Show real people using your product or service or share your brand's origin story. Make your audience laugh, cry, or feel inspired; emotions are the glue that makes your message memorable. Embrace the power of your audience. Run contests and use hashtags to encourage them to share their stories. Their perspectives enrich your brand narrative and showcase its local impact. This means celebrating together. Share your company's successes and milestones but also celebrate your audience's wins. Acknowledge their achievements related to your brand and show appreciation for their support.

Visuals are your global language. Use high-quality images and videos that grab attention and reflect your brand's unique identity. Incorporate local flavor for the African market while maintaining an internationally appealing aesthetic. Collaborate with local photographers, videographers, and designers to capture the essence of your brand and connect with your audience on a deeper level. Additionally, partner with established figures in your industry for interviews, co-authored articles, or joint webinars. Leverage their reach while boosting your own credibility. By combining compelling visuals with strategic collaborations, you can create a powerful brand experience that resonates with people across cultures.

Your personal brand is the foundation of your business success. However, building a strong brand takes consistent effort. By investing time and effort into building a strong personal brand, you'll not only differentiate yourself from the competition but also inspire others to join your journey. Implementing these tactics and staying true to your brand identity will help you craft a powerful social media presence that resonates with audiences in Africa and around the world. You'll not only connect but also establish yourself as a thought leader in your industry. The world is waiting to hear your voice.

Embracing lifelong learning

As I mentioned previously, I'm a professor's daughter. On top of that, I'm a *Nigerian* professor's daughter, which means my drive to learn everything, know everything, be everything, has been cultivated from a very young age. Thankfully, I not only love to read, but I've also always been a very fast reader. I see the same now in my younger son, who also – as a delightful surprise to me, especially after his initial grumbling – became a voracious reader at the tender age of seven. Unlike his older brother, who struggled at the same age to get through the thirty-minute mandatory reading allotment each day, my younger son will beg me for another hour, perhaps even two, to read long into the night. I am hopeful that this will turn into the same thirst for knowledge that his mother has.

Constantly connecting with, teaching, and inspiring your audience requires you to increase your own knowledge.

Cultivating a culture of continuous learning – whether in yourself, your household, or your company – comes down to one thing: curiosity. What are you curious about? How eager are you to find out whether that new factoid is really true? Do you love languages? Numbers? Facts? Each of us are motivated by distinct types of knowledge, and, given the world we live in today, we thankfully have the flexibility to pursue that knowledge in a way that suits us. I go back to my love of reading – this means that, rather than listening to podcasts or watching documentaries, I am much more likely to buy a book on the subject, whether I read it myself or turn to the efficiency of audiobooks. There's a depth that can be achieved in those two to three hundred pages that just can't be reached within even an hour-long podcast. So, I read, I underline, I highlight, I read again.

Of course, as my free time continues to drop dramatically with the addition of two kids, then running a business, and now building my own business, I have turned to articles, blogs, and sometimes even targeted videos to fill that gap. The world is changing every day, and the only way to remain in place, talk less of getting ahead, is to keep learning. Whether it's about generative artificial intelligence (AI), the Kenyan tech scene, or even the latest Netflix show in Africa, I need to remain abreast of what's happening around me, focusing on global business trends and market dynamics.

However, I also avoid learning just for the sake of learning. I'm not a professor, after all, just the daughter of one. If I don't implement my learning into my own business and supporting my own clients, the learning becomes less useful. My learning is the most productive when I can speak to an insurtech CEO in the USA about what another insurtech CEO is doing in South Africa; or describe to a cohort of emerging fund managers the best practice governance procedures I have seen in play across continents; or partner with a South Africa-based organization to bring a message drafted in the West but shaped on the African continent to Nigeria. This all comes from the power of leveraging global best practices. Yes, I've said that West is not always best – however, we all have something to learn from each other.

Here's how to pick up business hacks from all over the world without getting overwhelmed:

- **Watch the winners:** See what's working for businesses like yours in other countries. Research industry reports, attend online conferences (think: free webinars), or chat with international business folks.

- **Think local first:** Don't copy everything. Ask yourself if that fancy new marketing trick from Japan would fly with your local customers. Consider things like laws, what people like, and how your competitors play the game.

- **Make it your own:** For the good stuff that fits your local scene, bend it a bit. Maybe a product needs a tweak or your customer service approach could use a global-inspired upgrade.

The thing is, there's no one-size-fits-all approach to global expansion. The key lies in finding the right balance between global standardization and local personalization. You can opt for a global strategy with consistent elements like top-notch quality control but tailor your approach market by market, adjusting marketing campaigns and product features to suit local preferences, tastes, and rules. A hybrid model that combines standardized core processes with personalized customer experiences can also be effective. Experimentation is crucial; try out a couple of global best practices on a small scale. See how they perform with your local audience. Learn from your experiments and adjust before going all-in. Remember, the business landscape is constantly evolving, so stay curious and adaptable, and keep an eye on global trends and best practices so your local business stays ahead of the game.

This is how we can borrow smart ideas from around the world and make them work like a charm for our local business, finding the winning formula for us here in Africa.

Final thoughts

By embracing a global mindset, leveraging technology, and adapting to local markets, you can position your business for long-term success. It's time to step beyond borders and redefine what it means to be an African entrepreneur. Let's build a future where African businesses are not just competing globally but leading the way. Join me in Part Two, as we explore the defining elements of African excellence.

PART TWO
BUILDING AFRICAN EXCELLENCE

THREE

Defining African Excellence

I've already mentioned how much I love to read. I enjoy mostly fiction, specifically, detective stories, but in the spirit of continuous learning and personal development, I periodically and regularly force myself to read business books such as this one. There are a handful that I tend to recommend when people come to me, but just one that I read every year to renew its impact on my vision and life, and that's Gary Keller and Jay Papasan's *The ONE Thing: The Surprisingly Simple Truth About Extraordinary Results*. In *The ONE Thing*, Keller and Papasan argue that chasing after multiple goals is a recipe for mediocrity. Their premise is that true success hinges on identifying your single most important goal – your ONE Thing. This ONE Thing, they argue, should be the core of your purpose and drive everything you do. Re-reading their book each January continues to dismantle my own misconceptions about productivity, for example, that multitasking is the key to getting things done. Instead, they advocate for a laser-sharp focus on ONE Thing at a time. I've introduced their so-called "focusing question" – "What is the ONE Thing I can do such that by doing it everything else will be easier or unnecessary?" (Keller and Papasan, 2013) – into my own planning to help me prioritize more ruthlessly and identify the actions that will have the biggest domino effect on my goals.

My ONE Thing is Africa. More specifically, it's building the new Africa so that my sons grow up as proud global Africans. With this as my ONE Thing, both my business *and* my life revolve around building a future where not only my sons but all African youth can thrive. Money, including profit, has never been much of a motivating factor for me. While I enjoy the periods when I don't have to think twice before buying the latest handbag from my favorite Ibadan-based leather handbag designer, uplifting my continent and creating opportunities for others have always been central to me. I understand the importance of leadership in this endeavor, which is why I tend to prioritize the importance of building strong teams and fostering leadership among our companies and people. Returning to my homeland was always the north star guiding my decisions, whether personal or professional. I have unwittingly left many guys behind once I understood that their life path didn't coincide with my African pride and urge to return home. Now, every single day, I'm immensely delighted to be, through my sons, vicariously living the childhood that I never got – not in terms of material things, but through the opportunity to be surrounded by people who look like me, who know and are proud of their identity as Africans.

As we continue to talk about African excellence, I hope that I've been a true model of what that means through the perfectionism that pushes me to be the best, and, even more importantly, deliver the best. That same perfectionism drives me to re-read that email for the third time, to open each attachment before pressing the send button, to find every error in even the smallest PowerPoint, to make sure I turn up thirty minutes early to every meeting. As they say, actions speak louder than words, and I must embody my vision for the future Africa and the "real Nigerian" in every action that I take, and hope and pray for the butterfly effect that will perhaps inspire hundreds, and through them, millions. Essentially, my business and life have become intertwined, each step contributing to a stronger, more vibrant Africa for my sons and future generations.

Turning your ONE Thing into a business

I talk about delivering excellence and African excellence all the time. But what does this excellence look like? And how can we leverage the butterfly effect by helping others to deliver it? Delivering excellence in the context of building a new Africa shares some core characteristics with delivering excellence anywhere, but we also need to incorporate a few unique African values:

- Ubuntu-inspired collaboration
- Resourceful innovation
- Sustainable impact

Ubuntu-inspired collaboration

This value combines customer service and collaboration, drawing inspiration from the African philosophy of Ubuntu (*oo-boon-too*). Ubuntu emphasizes the interconnectedness of humanity (i.e., the essence of being human) and the importance of community. Its core principle – "I am because we are" – emphasizes collective identity and mutual responsibility. The philosophy of Ubuntu originates from the Bantu languages of Southern Africa, particularly among the Nguni people of present-day South Africa, Zimbabwe, and Mozambique. While Ubuntu is rooted in Southern African cultures, similar communal philosophies exist across the African continent, such as Ujamaa in East Africa and Ma'at in ancient Egypt. It also exists in other parts of the world, as the core principles of human interdependence, community solidarity, and collective responsibility find resonance in various indigenous philosophies globally. These shared values across cultures highlight the universal human yearning for social cohesion and mutual care.

Now, let's talk business. Imagine a company where everyone feels valued, where *teamwork* isn't just a buzzword, but a way of life. That's Ubuntu in action. It's about understanding that your success is intertwined with the success of your team, your customers, and your community. It's about putting people first, building trust, and working together toward a common goal. It's about recognizing that we're all in this together, and that by lifting each other up, we all rise.

Resourceful innovation

Resourceful innovation merges innovation with the quintessential African spirit of resourcefulness. Here, the focus is on solving challenges – both for your business and your customers – with creativity and a keen eye for what's available. We know that we often have limited resources, but these can become the springboard for ingenious solutions (i.e., thinking locally to create brilliantly).

Resourceful innovation thrives on understanding the unique context of Africa. Instead of copying existing models, it prioritizes designing products and services that are specifically affordable, accessible, and culturally relevant. By adapting existing technologies, or even creating entirely new ones using what's readily available, resourceful innovation empowers Africans to solve African challenges.

Therefore, you need to get the most out of what you have, creating high-quality solutions that are affordable for your target market. This doesn't mean sacrificing quality; it means being smart. You might utilize open-source technologies, simplify product designs, or explore innovative distribution channels to keep costs down. Think like MacGyver and encourage your team to do the same. Ask yourself: Can everyday objects be used in new ways to solve problems? Are there alternative production methods that are more cost-effective? By embracing a resourceful mindset, you can stretch your resources further and deliver excellent value and become a leader in creating African solutions for African challenges. This approach not only benefits African businesses but also fosters a culture of self-reliance and ingenuity within the continent.

Sustainable impact

Sustainable impact isn't about short-term wins; it's about building a thriving future for Africa, and it goes beyond just the environment. It means ensuring your business practices are both environmentally and socially responsible and embrace good governance. Focus on creating a positive impact in the communities you serve. This could involve creating jobs through local hiring and training programs, supporting local education initiatives to empower future generations, or promoting sustainable farming practices. Remember, success isn't just measured in profits. A key metric should be the positive change you create for future generations. By fostering economic development, social good, and environmental responsibility, you build a legacy that extends far beyond your bottom line.

Remember, though, that sustainable impact also requires embracing good governance practices. This means operating with transparency and accountability, ensuring ethical decision-making throughout your organization. Fair treatment of employees, fair wages, and a commitment to safety should be cornerstones of your business practices. Ultimately, good governance strengthens your reputation, attracts responsible investors, and paves the way for long-term sustainable growth that benefits all stakeholders. By operating with transparency, accountability, and a commitment to ethical practices, your business can become a role model for good governance in Africa, inspiring a future where businesses are not just profitable but also forces for positive change.

Prioritizing the values of Ubuntu-inspired collaboration, resourceful innovation, and sustainable impact allows us to build businesses that contribute to a thriving new Africa for not just our individual circles, but countless others. By weaving these characteristics together, we can build businesses that embody African excellence.

Attracting the dream client for your ONE Thing

The most critical realization I've had since hitting my forties is finally accepting that I'm not for everyone – and that I don't have to be. My internal mantra has become "Take me as I am." In the same way, not every client (or customer) will be right for you when you are building African excellence. Clients who resonate with the values of African excellence will be ideal partners for your business. These dream clients will get you out of bed in the morning, excited to tackle new challenges. In fact, they aren't just clients; they're partners in building a better Africa. They're the ones who see the big picture. They get that success isn't just about profits; it's about impact. They're passionate about our continent, its people, and its potential. They're not afraid to roll up their sleeves and get their hands dirty. They understand that *Ubuntu* isn't just a word; it's a way of doing business.

Imagine working with someone who shares your vision for a thriving Africa. Someone who sees your business as a force for good. That's the kind of client who will inspire you to reach new heights. Collaborating with clients who are passionate about African excellence allows you to not only deliver excellent service but also create a ripple effect of positive change across the continent. But how do you find these dream clients?

Attracting clients who embody the values of African excellence requires a strategic approach that goes beyond traditional marketing tactics. Here's how I connect with purpose-driven partners across diverse African markets:

- **I leverage impact networks:** I move beyond the large standard industry conferences to seek out smaller events and organizations specifically focused on social good and sustainable development in Africa. Speaking at these events demonstrates my alignment with their values and positions me as a trusted partner. Partnering with organizations like Shared Value Africa, based in South Africa, allows me to connect with a pre-qualified pool of clients who share my commitment to building a better future.

- **I act as a thought leader:** I've established myself as an expert in my field by continuously sharing my knowledge and expertise through thought leadership initiatives, contributing articles, and hosting webinars on challenges faced by African businesses, including my monthly newsletter, "Adeolu the Afro-optimist." Additionally, the digital landscape offers me a wealth of opportunities to build online communities of impact via, for example, WhatsApp.

- **I speak the language of shared values:** I tailor my messaging to resonate with my dream client's values. Rather than using generic marketing speak, I craft narratives that connect with these clients' aspirations for Africa's future. This may mean incorporating greater transparency in their promotion process, helping them to strengthen their leadership team, or expanding their influence within the healthcare ecosystem.

By implementing one, two, or all of these strategies, you can shift your focus from transactional sales to building genuine connections with purpose-driven clients. This approach will not only attract your dream clients but also foster a network of collaborators who share your vision for a thriving Africa. Remember, your dream client is looking for more than just a product or service; they're seeking a partner on their journey toward a brighter future for our continent.

Leveraging the excellence of the diaspora

It was the end of 2022, and I had recently left my CEO role at a global multinational with the intention of taking a career break like the one I had taken before joining the same company eleven years earlier. However, unlike before, when I spent the majority of my break on a beach in south Turkey with a Kindle in hand, I knew that this one was going to be much more active, particularly as, with two young children in tow, I no longer had the luxury of completely shutting down from society. So I started looking around for ways to better inform my transition from a life as a corporate drone to one of purpose and fulfillment. And, lo and behold, I stumbled across a conference I'd never heard of all the way on the west side of the USA (I was based in Lagos, Nigeria) that seemed to speak to me. See, as someone whose parents had emigrated away from her birthland when she wasn't even three, I had from very early on been a part of the nebulous "diaspora." So when I stumbled across the African Diaspora Investment Summit (ADIS), I thought, "Perfect, I need to be there." I booked my ticket, packed my bags, and headed over to the USA to learn more about why and how the African diaspora was so great and necessary to our success as a continent.

But first, what is the African diaspora? The term refers to the global communities descended from the historic migrations of peoples from Africa, particularly since the fifteenth century. It encompasses both voluntary and involuntary movements, including the transatlantic slave trade, which was the largest forced migration of Africans to the Americas. The term *African diaspora* first appeared in the literature in the 1950s and broadly includes all global communities descended from historic migrations of Africans. The African diaspora continues to play a vital role in global socio-economic and cultural dynamics, and organizations like the African Diaspora Network (the conveners of ADIS) aim to activate capital and resources from the diaspora for the development of Africa and communities worldwide.

While precise numbers are difficult due to the diaspora's global spread, credible estimates put the total African diaspora population at around 350 million people dispersed across the Americas, Europe, the Middle East, and other regions (SOAD, n.d.). This makes it one of the largest diasporic populations in the world, stemming from both historic forced migration and more recent voluntary movements. Here are some key details on the size of the African diaspora (The Diaspora Collective, 2019):

- It is considered the third-largest population in the world after China and India, larger than the USA, Indonesia, and Brazil.

- In the Americas alone, there are approximately 113 million people of African descent living in Latin America, 39 million in North America, and 14 million in the Caribbean.

- In Europe, there are around 4 million people of African descent.

- The transatlantic slave trade forcibly moved between 12 and 14 million enslaved Africans to the Americas between the sixteenth and nineteenth centuries. Their descendants make up a sizable portion of the modern African diaspora.

- The African Union (n.d.) defines the African diaspora broadly as "people of native or partial African origin living outside the continent, irrespective of their citizenship and nationality."

But back to ADIS... what did I learn? I learned that the diaspora represents a vast pool of talent with expertise across various industries and about ways to partner with diaspora organizations and online platforms to connect with skilled professionals eager to contribute to Africa's growth. These professionals can provide valuable knowledge transfer and mentorship opportunities, fostering innovation and propelling businesses forward. I also learned that the diaspora holds immense marketing potential and that I could partner with successful members of the diaspora who could become brand ambassadors for my company. Their stories about connecting with their African roots and contributing to the continent's progress resonates with potential clients who share those values, creating a powerful marketing narrative that showcases my commitment to African excellence. In this way, they could showcase the positive change my business brings to Africa, attracting the diaspora as investors, partners, or even returnees. Finally, I learned that many within the diaspora have a fervent desire to support African ventures, and that a number utilize diaspora crowd-funding platforms to raise capital for their businesses. As these platforms cater specifically to projects focused on African development, they allow us to tap into an enthusiastic investor base who believe in our mission. By effectively engaging the diaspora through these strategies, we gain access to skilled human capital, enthusiastic brand advocates, and potential investors – all critical ingredients for building a thriving business that contributes to a new Africa. Transparency and good governance are essential to assure the diaspora and its members' contributions are used responsibly.

I also learned at ADIS that the Indian diaspora, which has similar population numbers globally, offers a blueprint for engaging the African diaspora in Africa's development. Skilled Indian professionals abroad, through brain circulation or remote work, strengthen India's human capital. Many diaspora members establish businesses in their host countries, and some invest back in India, bringing not just capital but valuable business experience. The Indian diaspora is a major source of foreign direct investment, fueling innovation and growth.

Closer to home, Ghana recognized the potential of the diaspora early on. In 2000, it enacted the Citizenship Act, allowing Ghanaians abroad to retain their citizenship and enjoy rights like property ownership. This move fostered a stronger connection between Ghanaians abroad and in their homeland. Building on this foundation, Ghana established the Diaspora Affairs Office (n.d.) within the Office of the President in 2017. This dedicated office focuses on initiatives to attract investment, bridge the skills gap, facilitate knowledge sharing, and, finally, promote "diaspora tourism." Ghana's Diaspora Engagement Policy, launched in 2023, further emphasizes the importance of collaboration (IOM, 2023). It aims to create a mutually beneficial relationship in which the diaspora contributes to Ghana's development, while Ghana fosters a welcoming environment for their return and engagement.

By leveraging the teachings from ADIS and emulating Ghana's and India's examples, African countries can unlock the immense potential of their diaspora communities, paving the way for African businesses to unlock the immense potential of the African diaspora to drive growth and build a new Africa.

Building strategic and sustainable excellence: The SCALE framework

As we discussed previously, the spirit of African excellence is a relentless pursuit of excellence. The recovering perfectionist in me takes immense pride in her work and aspires to deliver the absolute best. However, this dedication isn't just about personal achievement; it's about setting a powerful example, rewriting a false narrative, and hopefully inspiring not just hundreds, but millions to strive for a brighter future. And that's exactly what African excellence is all about. Your business can also be a shining example of African excellence, and to help you turn that vision into reality, I've developed a five-step roadmap to transformation. Let's turn your passion for African excellence into a tangible roadmap for success through the SCALE framework:

- Strategize your vision

- Champion excellence

- Accelerate exceptional leadership

- Leverage governance for sustainable growth

- Expand your impact via growth capital

We'll go over each part of the framework in detail in the following chapters, but first, let's look at the big picture.

S – Strategize your vision

Develop a comprehensive business strategy focused on scalability and sustainability. Create a clear roadmap outlining your business goals, target market, growth strategies, and financial projections. Utilize both quantitative and qualitative data to understand your target audience and their needs and preferences. Leverage technology to gather and analyze competitor and market trends. Clearly articulate the unique value your business offers to customers and how it addresses their pain points. Utilize storytelling to connect emotionally with your target audience. Implement your strategic roadmap with precision and operational efficiency. Design your business operations to accommodate growth. Consider factors such as technology, infrastructure, HR, and supply chain to ensure scalability. Establish measurable targets to track progress and evaluate the effectiveness of your strategies. Partner with consultants, mentors, or industry experts to gain valuable insights and support. Be prepared to pivot your strategy as market conditions change. Embrace a culture of experimentation and continuous improvement.

C – Champion excellence

Assemble and champion a team that reflects the diversity of your target market and brings a wide range of perspectives and experiences. Provide opportunities for employees to grow and develop their skills through training, mentorship, and coaching. Encourage experimentation, risk-taking and problem-solving, creating a space where innovative ideas and solutions can flourish. Delegate authority and responsibility, allowing employees to take ownership of their work and contribute to your company's success. Utilize employee engagement surveys to gather feedback and identify areas for improvement.

A – Accelerate exceptional leadership

Seek and provide leadership coaching to enhance decision-making skills and governance. Demonstrate the values of Ubuntu through your own actions and behaviors. Build trust and credibility by being transparent and authentic. Cultivate trust and open communication with employees, customers, partners, and stakeholders. Encourage continuous learning, adaptability, and resilience.

L – Leverage governance for sustainable growth

Regardless of your company's size, leverage a clear governance structure to protect and grow your business. Define roles and responsibilities, ensuring accountability and transparency. Create a governance structure that supports your business strategy and values. Integrate environmental, social, and governance (ESG) factors into decision-making. Develop a sustainability strategy aligned with your business goals. Collaborate with governments, nongovernmental organizations (NGOs), and stakeholders to create shared value. Adhere to relevant regulations and industry standards to maintain a strong reputation. Conduct regular risk assessments and implement mitigation strategies.

E – Expand your impact via growth capital

Facilitate market expansion by driving networking and partnership opportunities, whether via organic (reinvested profit) or inorganic (external funding) sources. Build social capital by attending industry events, participating in trade missions, and building relationships with key stakeholders. Identify and secure appropriate funding channels to fuel growth. Develop a compelling investment pitch to attract potential investors. Create a clear roadmap for financial sustainability and growth. Utilize financial modeling to project future performance and make informed decisions. Track KPIs to monitor progress and make data-driven decisions. Use analytics to identify trends and opportunities for improvement.

Your dedication to excellence – that relentless drive to get things right – isn't just about you; it's about the powerful ripple effect you can create. Imagine inspiring hundreds – even millions – to embrace the same principles of collaboration, innovation, and sustainability. That's the true essence of African excellence, and it's within your reach. Implementing the SCALE framework will equip you to be the change you want to see. It's your blueprint to transform your venture into a shining example for Africa, a beacon that illuminates a path to a thriving future. But remember, this roadmap isn't a rigid set of instructions. It's a springboard to spark your creativity and strategic thinking. As you navigate the unique landscape of African markets, be ready to adapt and refine your approach.

Final thoughts

The beauty of African excellence lies in its focus on shared success. You won't be building your business in a vacuum. By fostering a collaborative spirit within your team, partnering with local communities, and leveraging the expertise of the African diaspora, you'll be building a powerful ecosystem where everyone benefits. Here's the most exciting part: you have the potential to become a magnet, attracting dream clients who share your values. These are clients who understand that success isn't just about profit; it's about creating positive social and environmental change. Together, we can build a movement that transcends individual companies, inspiring a new generation of African entrepreneurs to embrace purpose alongside profit.

This journey won't be easy. There will be challenges, but with a commitment to continuous improvement and a relentless pursuit of excellence, you'll overcome them. Are you ready to answer the call? Though the SCALE framework is your guide, the real power lies in your hands.

Before we dig deeper into each step in the following chapters, complete the scorecard at https://zerconsulting.com/scaleyourbusiness to evaluate where you currently fall on the SCALE.

FOUR

S – Strategize Your Vision

For all the times that I've used the expression "culture eats strategy for breakfast," I've thought at least twice the time about the equally familiar saying "if you fail to plan, you plan to fail." And what is a business strategy if not a plan for your business?

Crafting your strategic blueprint

Just like a solid foundation is crucial for building a house, a well-crafted strategy is the bedrock of a thriving business. It provides a clear roadmap for achieving your goals, allocating resources effectively, and making informed decisions. In this section, we will explore the key elements of a comprehensive business strategy focused on scalability and sustainability:

1. Crafting your strategic blueprint

   – **Phase 1**: Strategy assessment and visioning

   – **Phase 2**: Goal setting and strategic objectives

2. Executing your strategic plan

   – **Phase 3**: Strategy development and execution planning

   – **Phase 4**: Communication and stakeholder engagement

Phase 1: Strategy assessment and visioning

Outcome: A shared vision for the future, a clear and concise mission statement, and a deep understanding of your market, customers, and competitive landscape.

Phase 1 involves laying the groundwork for your strategic blueprint. We'll start by defining your purpose, vision, tenets, and values (PVTV), which will serve as the north star for your business. Next, we'll conduct a comprehensive market analysis to understand your target audience, competitive landscape, and industry trends. Finally, we'll develop a scalable and sustainable business model that outlines how you will create, deliver, and capture value.

1. Define your PVTV

Your business is more than just a profit-making machine. It's about purpose, vision, values, and the guiding principles that shape your decisions. Your PVTV is your business's purpose – its heart and soul. Your *purpose* is about defining why your business exists, what problem it solves for your customers, and the impact you want it to make on the world. Your *vision* is the compass that guides your journey. It's about envisioning where you want to be in five or ten years and what success looks like for your business. Your *tenets* are the guiding principles that shape your decisions, and your *values* are the bedrock of your company culture. This PVTV guides every decision you make. It should be clear, inspiring, and something your team can rally behind.

2. Conduct a comprehensive market analysis

Once you have a clear understanding of your PVTV, it's time to start thinking about your market. Understanding your market means knowing your customers inside and out. It's about understanding their needs, wants, and pain points. It's about knowing who your competitors are and how you can stand out. And it's about staying ahead of the curve by understanding the latest trends in your industry. Knowing your customers is like knowing your family: you understand their needs, their wants, and what keeps them up at night. That's why understanding your market is so crucial. Who are your ideal customers? What challenges do they face? How can you break your market into smaller groups to better understand each one's specific needs? Next, take a good look at the competition. Who are your rivals? What are they doing well? Where do they fall short?

This is your chance to find your unique selling point – what sets you apart from the crowd. Finally, keep your eyes on the prize by looking at the big picture. What's happening in your industry? Are new trends emerging? How can you stay ahead of the curve and use these trends to your advantage?

3. Develop a scalable and sustainable business model

Your business model is your blueprint for making money. It's about creating, delivering, and capturing value. But it's not just about today; it's about tomorrow too. Your business model should be able to grow and adapt. Start with your unique value proposition. What makes your business special? How do you solve problems for your customers in a way that no one else can? This is your secret sauce – the reason people choose you over your competitors. Next, think about how you'll bring in the cash. What's your pricing strategy? How will you attract new customers and keep them coming back? Remember, it's not just about making money; it's about managing your costs. Where can you cut back without hurting your business? Remember, your business model is a living document. You should review it regularly to ensure it's still working for you.

To achieve the outcomes in Phase 1, you will:

- Assess your core competencies, resources, and capabilities across defined asset categories

- Conduct a gap analysis between your current and desired future states using tools like online assessments, scorecards, and surveys

- Review your findings against an external analysis of the industry landscape to identify potential opportunities and threats

By the end of Phase 1, you will have a clear picture of your business's strengths, weaknesses, opportunities, and threats (SWOT), as well as a shared vision for the future. This foundation will be essential for developing a winning strategy in the subsequent phases.

Phase 2: Goal setting and strategic objectives

Outcome: Specific KPIs to track progress toward investment readiness, with a clear focus on achieving desired outcomes.

Now that you have a clear vision for your business and a deep understanding of your market, Phase 2 will help you set your sights on achieving your goals and turn your vision into a reality with actionable goals and a strategic roadmap to achieve them.

1. Set clear and measurable goals

Imagine your goals as milestones on your journey. They guide your progress and keep you focused. So what do you want to achieve? Whether it's increasing revenue, expanding your market, or improving customer satisfaction, setting clear and measurable goals is essential. Think about what truly matters to your business. Do you want to boost your bottom line? Improve operational efficiency? Or are you focused on winning over more customers? Let's break it down:

- **Financial goals:** What's your target revenue? How much profit do you want to make? What's your growth rate?

- **Operational goals:** How efficient are your operations? What are the key metrics that show how well you're running your business?

- **Customer goals:** How many new customers do you want to acquire? How can you keep your existing customers happy?

2. Develop a strategic roadmap

Your strategic roadmap is your GPS, guiding you from point A to point B. It's a clear plan of action that outlines the steps you'll take to reach your goals. What are the most important projects or initiatives you need to focus on? When should you start and finish each one? What resources do you need to make it happen? And most importantly, how will you measure your progress? Your strategic roadmap is a living document that outlines the steps you will take to achieve your goals. It should be clear, concise, and easy to understand.

3. Harness the power of data

In today's world, data is your secret weapon. By collecting and analyzing data, you can gain valuable insights into your customers, your market, and your business performance. What information do you need to make informed decisions? How can you collect this data efficiently? Once you have it, how can you turn it into actionable insights? Technology is your ally in this journey. There are tools out there that can help you collect, analyze, and visualize your data.

To achieve the outcomes in Phase 2, you will:

- Identify key strategic goals that align with your PVTV

- Develop specific, measurable, achievable, relevant, and time-bound (SMART) objectives for each strategic goal

- Define an ideal investment timeline to guide your strategic planning and resource allocation

- Evaluate potential future investors to identify their strategic fit and align your goals accordingly

By the end of Phase 2, you will have a clear set of goals and a detailed plan for achieving them, along with the necessary metrics to track your progress toward investment readiness.

An ongoing process

Crafting a winning strategy is not a one-time event. It's an ongoing process that requires continuous monitoring, evaluation, and adjustment. By following the steps outlined in this section, you can develop a sturdy foundation for your business and set yourself up for long-term success. In the next section, we will step through Phases 3 and 4, further exploring how to translate a strategy into actionable steps, including setting goals, allocating resources, planning operations, and setting up performance metrics.

Executing your strategic plan

A well-crafted strategy is essential, but its true value lies in execution. Turning your strategic vision into reality requires meticulous planning, operational efficiency, and a relentless focus on delivering results. In this section, we'll explore how to translate your strategy into actionable steps, build a high-performance team, and create a culture of execution.

Phase 3: Strategy development and execution planning

Outcome: Detailed action plans, a robust performance measurement system, and an effective reporting mechanism to track progress and inform decision-making.

Now that you have a clear roadmap, Phase 3 will help you turn your strategy into action. This phase is about turning your vision into reality, measuring your progress, and making sure you're on track.

1. Design for scale

Imagine your business as a car. You've got a great roadmap, but now you need a vehicle that can handle the journey. This is where building a scalable business comes in. Technology is your copilot. Invest in tools that can manage the workload as your business grows. Think of cloud-based systems, automation, and data analytics as your autopilot, helping you navigate challenges smoothly. Your infrastructure is the chassis, or frame, of your operations. Make sure your facilities and supply chain can keep up with increasing demands. That's like ensuring your car has enough fuel and a reliable engine. People are your driving force. Invest in your team, create a workplace where innovation thrives, and watch your business accelerate. Finally, keep your finances healthy. Strong financial systems are like a well-maintained car. Regular check-ups and proper care will help you manage your growth and avoid unexpected breakdowns. By carefully considering these factors, you can create an organization that is well-positioned to capitalize on growth opportunities.

2. Set the pace

Your KPIs are your business dashboard, filled with dials and gauges that show you how you're doing. They're the numbers that tell you if you're on the right track. Start by looking at the financial side of your business. How's your revenue looking? Are you profitable? Are you making a good return on your investments? Remember, cash is king, so keep an eye on your cash flow. Next, look at how smoothly your operations are running. Are you productive? Do you deliver quality products or services? And most importantly, are your customers happy? Finally, measure your growth. How many new customers are you bringing on board? Are you gaining market share? Are your customers sticking around? Remember, numbers don't lie. Use your KPIs to understand what's working and what needs improvement. It's like checking your car's dashboard to see if you need to refuel or make a pit stop.

3. Adapt to succeed

Africa is a vibrant, diverse continent with unique opportunities and challenges. To succeed, you need a strategy tailored to this dynamic landscape. Start by truly understanding your customers. What do African consumers want and need? How do their buying habits differ from those in other markets? Armed with this knowledge, you can create products and services that resonate. Building strong partnerships is also key. Collaborate with local businesses, government agencies, and communities. Together, you can create win-win situations that benefit everyone. Technology can be a powerful tool for overcoming Africa's unique challenges. Explore how innovation can improve access to your products or services. Finally, invest in local talent. A skilled workforce with a deep understanding of the market is invaluable. By nurturing local talent, you're not just building your business; you're contributing to the growth of the African economy.

To achieve the outcomes in Phase 3, you will:

- Develop detailed plans for each strategic objective
- Assign responsibilities, set deadlines, and allocate resources
- Establish a robust performance measurement system to track KPIs
- Develop a regular reporting mechanism to communicate performance

By the end of Phase 3, you will have a clear, actionable plan to execute your strategic plan so that your business is scalable and adaptable, whatever the circumstances.

Phase 4: Communication and stakeholder engagement

Outcome: Internal and external understanding and support of your strategy, leading to increased buy-in and successful implementation.

Getting everyone on board is crucial for success. Phase 4 is about sharing your vision, building support, and fostering a sense of ownership across your organization.

1. Get everyone on board

Effective communication is key to success. Share your vision with the world. Craft your story, developing a compelling narrative that captures the essence of your strategy. Share your vision with your team in a clear and inspiring way. Use various channels to reach everyone. Build strong relationships with investors, partners, and customers. Let them know what you're doing and why it matters. Remember, your team and stakeholders are your partners in this journey. Involve them, listen to their ideas, and build a shared sense of purpose.

2. Focus on what matters

Not every idea is a winner. Focus on the projects that will really move the needle. First, make sure every project aligns with your overall goals. Is the project taking you closer to your vision? If not, it might be time to reconsider. Next, weigh your options. Which projects have the biggest potential impact on your business? Be realistic; you can't do everything. Use your resources wisely. Spread yourself too thin, and you risk not achieving your full potential. Focus on what matters most. Finally, anticipate challenges. What could go wrong? By identifying potential risks upfront, you can develop strategies to overcome them.

3. Build a culture of execution

Your team is your greatest asset. Create a workplace where everyone feels valued, empowered, and excited to come to work. Open communication is key. Share information openly, be transparent, and make sure everyone understands the big picture and their role in it. Empower your team to make decisions and take ownership of their work. Trust them to do their jobs and watch their confidence soar. Celebrate successes and show appreciation for hard work. A little recognition goes a long way in boosting morale and motivation. Finally, invest in your team's growth. Offer opportunities for learning and development. When your team grows, your business grows.

To achieve the outcomes in Phase 4, you will:

- Prepare a final strategy document, including an executive summary, strategic objectives, action plans, and financial projections

- Develop a communication plan to disseminate your strategy

- Communicate your new strategy both internally and externally

At the end of Phase 4, you will have a team of dedicated, capable people working on projects that they believe in and that take your business closer to your goals.

Driving sustainable growth

Successful strategy execution requires meticulous planning, effective leadership, and a relentless focus on results. By following the steps outlined in this section, you can build a high-performance organization, create a culture of execution, and drive sustainable growth. However, the business landscape is constantly evolving. In the next section, we'll discuss the importance of agility and adaptability and explore strategies for navigating uncertainty and capitalizing on emerging opportunities.

Adapting and thriving

Your strategy isn't a static blueprint but a living document that evolves with the market. In today's rapidly changing landscape, businesses must be agile, adapting swiftly to new realities. For example, I once had a client who, despite a recent strategic review, found themselves adrift in a sea of altered market conditions. They sought my expertise to chart a new course, a process that culminated in a twelve-week sprint to redefine their growth trajectory. This is the essence of strategic agility – not just surviving change but thriving in its wake. Success hinges on your ability to identify emerging opportunities, assess risks, and execute with speed and precision. It's about more than simply reacting to change; it's about anticipating, shaping, and capitalizing on it. This is the reality of business in Africa, especially for small and midsize enterprises (SMEs). The pace of change is rapid, and your ability to adapt and pivot is crucial for survival and growth. It's like farming; you plant the seeds (strategy) and nurture them (execution), but you also need to be ready to adapt to unexpected weather conditions (market changes).

In dynamic African markets, where economic, technological, and social shifts are the norm, businesses must be prepared to pivot, experiment, and learn. One of the most significant challenges facing African businesses is the rapid pace of technological change. Digital disruption is transforming industries and creating new opportunities. It's essential to stay abreast of these trends and explore how you can leverage them to enhance your business model. For instance, consider how e-commerce, mobile payments, and generative AI can be integrated into your operations. But it's not just about technology. Economic shifts, political changes, and social trends can also disrupt your business. It's crucial to stay informed about these developments and be prepared to adjust your strategy accordingly. This means building a strong intelligence network, monitoring market trends, and conducting regular scenario planning exercises. Remember, failure is not the enemy; fear of failure is. Embracing a culture of experimentation and learning is essential for fostering innovation and adaptability. Encourage your team to try new things, take calculated risks, and learn from both successes and failures. Create a safe space for experimentation where people feel comfortable sharing ideas and taking ownership of projects. Another key aspect of adaptability is building strong relationships with your customers. By understanding their evolving needs and preferences, you can stay ahead of the curve and anticipate market shifts. Implement customer feedback mechanisms and use data analytics to gain insights into customer behavior.

Finally, it's essential to balance agility with strategic focus. While it's crucial to be adaptable, maintaining a clear vision is equally important. By defining your core values and long-term goals, you can ensure that your pivots align with your overall strategy. Adapting and thriving in the dynamic African market requires a combination of strategic thinking, operational agility, and a customer-centric mindset. By embracing change and continuously learning, you can position your business for long-term success. To foster a culture of adaptability, consider implementing these practices:

- **Regular strategic reviews:** Conduct periodic assessments of your strategy to identify areas for improvement and adaptation.

- **Quick decision-making:** Empower your team to make timely decisions in response to changing circumstances.

- **Scenario planning:** Develop plans for different potential future scenarios to prepare for various outcomes.

- **Continuous learning:** Invest in employee development to build a workforce equipped to manage change.

- **Experimentation:** Encourage a culture of experimentation and innovation.

- **Customer feedback loops:** Regularly seek feedback from customers to understand their evolving needs and adjust accordingly.

By integrating these practices into your business, you can enhance your ability to adapt to changing market conditions and seize new opportunities. Remember, your ability to pivot is not just a survival tactic; it's a strategic and competitive advantage.

Final thoughts

Crafting a winning strategy is akin to designing a roadmap to success. It requires careful planning, execution, and a relentless pursuit of adaptation. By following the steps outlined in this chapter, you've laid a solid foundation for your business journey. You've learned how to seed the future with a clear vision, cultivate growth through meticulous planning, and harvest abundance by embracing change.

Remember, a great strategy is essential, but it's the people who bring it to life. In Chapter 5, we'll explore the importance of cultivating a champion team – the cornerstone of any successful enterprise. By investing in your people, you'll unlock their potential and create a powerful force to drive your business forward.

FIVE

C – Champion Excellence

Africa's a land of audacious dreams. From bustling tech hubs to remote villages teeming with innovation, our continent is brimming with enterprising spirit. Some of us, and more each day, are turning those dreams into reality. We're creating groundbreaking solutions, disrupting industries, and shaping a brighter future for Africa. But here's the honest truth: even the most brilliant vision, the most meticulously crafted strategy, is just a collection of words on paper without the right people to execute it.

People as the cornerstone of African excellence

I was over a decade into my consulting career when I first had to build a team from scratch. Until then, I had been given already-formed teams to lead: a widely age-diverse team in Chicago, a tiny one-person team in Germany, and numerous expert project teams in between. However, when I transitioned to one of my German clients to drive the execution of a global change agenda across multiple regions, countries, and functions, it was initially just me. I couldn't wait to start until I had a team to back me, so I poured my heart, soul, and lots of time into hustling to keep all the various initiatives and projects moving. But the turning point came when I was finally able to pull together a small-but-mighty team of energetic, purposeful, and quite international individuals to push each of the CEOs and global leaders involved to execute our global vision. Together, my team of just five was a force to be reckoned with. With each of them hailing from different countries and with vastly different life experiences, they all provided a fresh perspective, challenged my assumptions, and helped me refine our approach. More importantly, they brought an infectious enthusiasm that fueled the entire team. That's the power of the right people. They're not just employees; they're co-conspirators in your audacious dream.

This isn't just my story. Statistics tell a clear story – a staggering percentage of African startups report talent as their biggest barrier to success. It's not a lack of funding, a bad market fit, or an imperfect product. It's picking the right individuals from underinvested educational systems and inadequate training programs, who can propel your venture forward. These startups spend countless hours on traditional recruitment methods – crafting perfect job descriptions, sifting through endless applications, and conducting interviews that leave hiring managers feeling drained. It's a time-consuming monster that can devour your energy, stealing precious focus from scaling your amazing venture. Worst of all is when, after all the time you spend hiring them, the person you bring in ends up not being the right fit, forcing you to begin the cycle all over again.

But what if there was a different path? Imagine attracting enthusiastic individuals who not only possess the skills you need but also share your vision for driving positive change in Africa. That's the power of strategic talent acquisition. In this chapter, we'll delve into the art and science of building a dream team in Africa. We'll explore strategies to navigate the unique talent landscape, identify top talent with a passion for development, and foster a culture that empowers individuals to excel. By the end of this chapter, you'll be equipped with the knowledge and tools to transform your talent search from a daunting task to an exciting adventure, attracting a team that will boost your venture and solidify the foundation of your African empire.

The African talent tightrope

Finding the right people here in Africa can feel like searching for gold in a haystack. It's not just about finding talent; it's about finding the right fit. You need people who share your vision, understand the African market, and are enthusiastic about making a difference. Let's talk about realities: you juggle a million things, from product development to customer service. Tackling recruitment head-on can feel like adding another ball to your already-overflowing basket. The competition for top talent is fierce. Established companies with deeper pockets and more established brands often have an edge. And the cultural complexity of Africa means there are different working styles and expectations across countries and regions. It's like trying to solve a complex puzzle while blindfolded.

But let's flip the script. What if these challenges were actually opportunities? What if, instead of seeing them as hurdles, we saw them as chances to build a truly exceptional team? That's where the magic happens. So let's turn this tightrope walk into a high-wire act. In the next section, we'll go over how to find your perfect match and build a dream team.

Finding your tribe

All right, so you're navigating the African talent tightrope, but how do you find those exceptional individuals who are the perfect fit for your team? Here's where we shift from dodging pitfalls to actively attracting the best. We want to find those rockstar professionals who not only possess the skills you need but also share your unwavering passion for developing Africa. Here are five key strategies to help you cast a wider net and attract your dream team:

1. **Think outside the job board:** Forget the usual online suspects. You need to go beyond generic job boards that might not reach the specific talent pool you crave. Instead, delve into the vibrant online communities frequented by young, Africa-focused professionals. Think industry associations buzzing with discussions, alumni networks of prestigious African universities brimming with bright minds, or online forums where innovation takes center stage. These communities are treasure troves waiting to be explored.

2. **Use your "why" as your superpower:** Don't underestimate the power of purpose. In today's world, people crave more than just a paycheck. Clearly articulate your company's mission and vision, but don't stop there. Emphasize how your work directly contributes to African development. Showcase your company's real-world impact and how each team member plays a crucial role in shaping a better future for the continent. This will resonate with those who share your passion for making a difference. If you can tell a compelling story about the "why" behind your business, you'll attract talented people who are driven by more than just a job title.

3. **Spotlight your culture:** Let your company culture shine through in everything you do, from your job descriptions to your social media presence. Craft descriptions that paint a vivid picture of your work environment, highlighting it as a space that fosters creativity, collaboration, and a shared commitment to making a positive impact. Showcase your company culture on your website and social media platforms. Share photos and stories that capture the energy and enthusiasm of your team. By letting your culture take center stage, you'll attract individuals who are a natural fit for your unique work environment.

4. **Get out there and network:** The world is your oyster – or should I say savanna? Don't be a passive observer. Industry conferences, pitch events, and innovation workshops are fantastic opportunities to connect with talented individuals who are enthusiastic about your field. Get involved! Participate in discussions, showcase your expertise, and actively network with potential candidates. Networking events are a goldmine for building relationships and identifying top talent who might not be actively searching for new opportunities.

5. **Use the power of storytelling:** Africa has a rich storytelling tradition, and you can leverage it to your advantage. Use case studies to illustrate your company's impact. Share employee

testimonials that highlight the personal and professional growth experienced within your team. Craft blog posts that showcase your team's journey and the positive change they're driving. By sharing these compelling stories, you'll attract individuals who want to be part of a meaningful adventure, not just another job. They'll see your company as a platform where they can contribute their skills and make a real difference alongside a passionate team.

Remember, recruiting top talent is about more than just checking boxes on a skills list. It's about finding those who share your vision, your values, and your unwavering dedication to developing Africa. By implementing these strategies, your search for talent can become an adventure that excites you and allows you to draw a talented, passionate team that will propel your business forward and help you achieve your goals for our continent.

Building a successful team

In the previous section, we talked about the importance of attracting the right people to your purpose and vision and why your team is the true cornerstone of your African business. Now, let's delve into the nitty-gritty of building your dream team – the beating heart that will propel your African venture forward.

Attracting top talent passionate about Africa

Forget the days of scrolling through generic job boards, hoping for a diamond in the rough. Africa's talent pool is a vibrant ecosystem teeming with potential, but you need to know where to cultivate connections. Here are some actions that go beyond the traditional methods, designed to help you find passionate individuals who are as fired up about Africa's potential as you are:

- **Think community, not just company:** Instead of a static job description, try fostering a conversation within a community of young, Africa-focused professionals. Industry associations buzzing with discussions about the latest advancements in your field; alumni networks of prestigious African universities where bright minds are constantly sparking new ideas; online forums where innovation takes center stage and passionate individuals debate solutions to Africa's challenges: these are gold mines waiting for you to explore them.

- **Engage, don't just advertise:** Hiring is not just about plastering your job description everywhere. Become an inspiration within the communities you're looking in. Craft a compelling narrative that goes beyond the typical mission statement. What is your company's story? What is the vision that keeps you up at night, brimming with excitement? How does your work directly impact Africa's development? Share this narrative on your website and social media platforms. Showcase your company culture – the energy, the collaboration, the shared purpose that defines your work environment. By letting your company's heart shine through, you'll attract talent that resonates with your values, not just the job title or bottom line.

- **Provide a homecoming for the diaspora:** Africa is on the rise, and the world is watching. Many talented professionals from the diaspora who have gained experience abroad now dream of returning home to contribute their skills and propel the continent forward. This presents a unique opportunity for you. Leverage your own network, and reconnect with former colleagues, friends, or family members who have ventured abroad for studies or work. Spread the word about the exciting opportunities you offer and the chance to be part of something bigger: the transformation of a continent. You might be surprised by the hidden gems you discover within your own network – individuals with a wealth of experience and a yearning to give back to their home.

- **Don't just fill positions; build relationships:** Remember, recruiting is a two-way street. By actively engaging with communities and fostering genuine connections, you're creating connections, not just hiring. This isn't a one-time interaction.

Offer guest lectures at universities, participate in online forums with industry experts, or host meet-and-greets specifically designed for African professionals looking to make a difference.

By becoming a thought leader within these communities, you'll establish your company as a magnet for top talent, a place where passionate individuals can contribute their skills and be part of something truly special.

Cultivating a diverse and thriving team

Africa's beauty transcends its breathtaking landscapes and vibrant cultures. It also lies in the rich tapestry of traditions, ethnicities, and perspectives that weave together to form the continent's unique identity. Embracing this diversity isn't just a feel-good notion; it's a strategic imperative for building a successful African venture. Here's how you can cultivate a team that reflects the richness of the continent it serves:

• **Champion inclusive recruitment:** Gone are the days of relying solely on traditional recruitment methods that often overlook hidden gems. Move beyond the usual job boards and actively seek out partnerships with organizations that empower underrepresented groups. Partner with initiatives focused on getting women into tech or youth development programs that nurture the next generation of African talent. By casting a wider net and fostering connections with diverse talent pools, you'll gain access to a broader range of perspectives and experiences.

- **Leverage the power of a diverse team:** Imagine a brainstorming session where each team member brings a unique perspective shaped by their background and experiences. A team that reflects the continent's diversity unlocks a treasure trove of creative solutions. A marketer from Ghana might understand the nuances of customer behavior in West Africa in ways someone else might miss. An engineer from Tanzania might approach a technical challenge with an entirely different viewpoint from one in Botswana, leading to a groundbreaking innovation. Diversity isn't just about checking boxes; it's about harnessing the collective power of a team that can see a problem from multiple angles and develop solutions that resonate with a wider audience.

- **Make culture supreme:** Let your company culture shine through in everything you do, from your job descriptions to your social media presence. Craft descriptions that paint a vivid picture of your work environment, highlighting a space that fosters creativity, collaboration, and a shared commitment to making a positive impact. Showcase your company culture on your website and social media platforms. Share photos and stories that capture the energy and enthusiasm of your team. By letting your culture take center stage, you'll attract individuals who are a natural fit for your unique work environment.

Aligning values and goals

Once you've cast a wider net and identified a pool of talented individuals from diverse backgrounds, here are some steps you can take to ensure they align with your company's vision and values:

- **Use storytelling:** Weave your company's story into the interview process. Don't just talk about the job description; talk about the mission that keeps you passionate, the challenges you're tackling, and the impact you dream of making. See if the candidate's eyes light up – that spark of genuine excitement is a sign of potential alignment. Someone who resonates with your mission is more likely to become an enthusiastic and dedicated team member, driven by a shared purpose that extends beyond a paycheck.

- **Uncover the person behind the paper:** Skills are important, but cultural fit is equally essential. Look for individuals who demonstrate a genuine passion for your company's goals and a willingness to collaborate effectively within a team environment. During the interview, delve deeper than the resume. Ask questions that uncover their motivations, work style, and desire to be part of a team working toward a bigger purpose.

- **Conduct a trial by project:** Consider incorporating a short-term (paid) internship or trial project (again, paid) into your recruitment process. These allow you to assess not just technical skills but also work ethic, communication style, and, most importantly, cultural fit. Think of this as a test drive: you get to see how the candidate operates within your team dynamic before making a permanent hiring decision. This allows you to assess not just technical skills but also softer skills that are crucial for building a cohesive and successful team.

Building a team that shines

Imagine a team where everyone feels like they belong, ideas flow freely, and diverse perspectives are celebrated. That's what we're aiming for: a team that's not just a collection of individuals, but a powerful force that reflects the vibrant tapestry of Africa. Diversity isn't just about ticking boxes; it's about harnessing different perspectives to create something extraordinary. It's about giving everyone a seat at the table and valuing their unique contributions. When we bring people together from divergent backgrounds, cultures, and experiences, magic happens. We spark innovation, solve problems in new ways, and build deeper connections with our customers. Remember, a team is more than just a group of people; it's a family. By fostering a sense of belonging and support, we create a space where everyone can thrive. Let's build teams that not only achieve business goals but also leave a positive impact on the ever-evolving continent we call home.

Investing in the future

Building a star team is one thing; keeping them motivated and engaged is another. Africa's dynamic business landscape demands a strategic approach to nurturing and retaining your team. It's like tending to a garden; you need the right conditions for your talent to flourish.

Tailoring rewards to build bridges

Let's talk about perks. While competitive salaries are crucial, in Africa's unique context, work is not just about the paycheck. Think beyond the basics – we're talking flexible working hours and remote options that accommodate long commutes or family needs. Health insurance that addresses common local concerns like malaria or maternity care demonstrates your commitment to your team's well-being. In some regions, mobile phone credit or transportation stipends can be highly valued benefits. But remember, it's not just about throwing money at problems. It's about understanding what truly motivates your people. And don't forget about recognition. Everyone loves a pat on the back. Celebrate wins, big and small. A simple "thank you" can go a long way. Publicly acknowledge achievements, and make sure your team feels valued.

But it's not just about the carrots. Sometimes, even as you embrace remote and hybrid work models, you need a little stick. Set clear expectations and performance metrics, provide regular feedback, and address performance issues head-on. A high-performing team needs structure and accountability, and a virtual one may need even more emphasis to maintain a sense of connection and collaboration. However, by mastering remote work strategies, you'll tap into a global talent pool and build a team that thrives in a flexible, dynamic work environment. Remember, your team is your greatest asset. Invest in them, nurture them, and watch your business bloom.

Honoring homegrown heroes and global mentors

Africa is brimming with talent. It's time we stop looking overseas for saviors and start investing in our own. We need to nurture local heroes and leverage the diaspora. When I came home to lead the subsidiary of a global multinational as CEO, I immediately brought in a well-seasoned expatriate who had a deep technical knowledge built within other emerging and African markets. However, I also ensured that my executive office was staffed with young, bright, local Nigerians who had been with the company from the beginning. This included an executive assistant recruited directly from our sales force to provide me with additional on-the-ground insight that I would otherwise have lacked, not having grown up in that market. In turn, I exposed my local team to the global best practices and practical apprenticeship that I'd received in my own early days.

That's the power of homegrown talent. They understand the market, they speak the language, and they're passionate about making a difference. Create opportunities for them to shine. Partner with universities, tech hubs, and vocational schools. Offer internships and apprenticeships. Build a pipeline of talent that's ready to take on the world. By investing in the future of African talent, you're not just building your team; you're contributing to the overall development of the continent's workforce.

But let's not forget our people in the diaspora. They have a wealth of knowledge and experience, and many yearn to contribute to Africa's development. Bring them back home, even if just for a little while. Offer remote work opportunities, mentorship programs, and chances to collaborate on projects. Create a bridge between the African continent and its global citizens. Engaging the diaspora is about building a powerful network that combines local expertise with global insights. It's about creating a future where our young people see endless possibilities and are excited to build their careers right here at home.

Securing the future

Africa is brimming with young talent, but raw potential needs guidance. We need to invest in the next generation of African leaders. It's not just about filling positions; it's about creating a legacy. Let's create a pipeline where our employees see a clear path for growth. Mentorship, coaching, and sponsorship should be the norm, not the exception.

Your company's success is tied to strong leadership. Don't wait for a crisis to hit before considering succession planning. Identify high-potential team members and invest in their leadership development. Provide opportunities for coaching, mentoring, and participation in leadership development programs. Implement mentorship programs that pair experienced team members with high-performing newcomers. This facilitates knowledge transfer, fosters a sense of community, and empowers the next generation of African business leaders. Don't limit yourself to internal mentorship, either. Seek out partnerships with established African entrepreneurs or industry experts who can share valuable insights and offer guidance specific to the African market. By building a strong leadership pipeline within your company, you ensure a smooth transition as your venture grows and evolves.

Building a dream team in Africa is an adventure – a constant process of learning, adapting, and growing together. Fostering a culture of innovation, resilience, and mutual investment will help you cultivate a team that becomes the driving force behind your venture's success. Remember, your people are the heart and soul of your African dream.

Igniting a culture of purpose

Let's talk about creating a workplace that feels more like a mission than a job. We need to build a team that's not just clocking in and out, but truly invested in what we're doing. This means inspiring people to bring their whole selves to work, not just their skills. Imagine a business where ideas flow freely, people feel empowered to take risks, and everyone is working toward a common goal. That's the kind of culture we want to create. It's about more than just perks and benefits; it's about giving people a sense of purpose.

Micromanagement is the enemy of innovation. Trust your team members and empower them to take ownership of their projects. Provide them with the resources and support they need to make data-driven decisions and see their ideas through to fruition. Encourage open communication and celebrate calculated risks. By creating a space where creativity flourishes, you'll unleash the full potential of your team and unlock groundbreaking solutions for your business.

Your team members should be driven not just by paychecks, but by a desire to make a difference. So help them see how their individual goals align with your company's mission. Regularly discuss your venture's impact and how your team's contributions make a positive change. Offer opportunities for professional development that align with their career aspirations.

By fostering a sense of purpose and growth, you'll ignite a passion within your team that fuels innovation and propels your company forward. For this reason, creating an exciting workplace is crucial. Foster an environment where people are challenged, supported, and celebrated, where they feel valued and empowered to make a difference. That's how you build a team that's not just good, but extraordinary.

Final thoughts

Building a successful African venture is about more than just profit. It's about creating a legacy – a positive impact that ripples through the continent. By investing in your people, fostering a culture of innovation and resilience, and empowering your team to reach their full potential, you're not just building a company; you're building a future for Africa. Your dream team will become a beacon of inspiration, paving the way for a new generation of entrepreneurs and shaping a brighter tomorrow for the continent.

Now, having assembled your world-class team, the next crucial step is to cultivate exceptional leadership within this team. In Chapter 6, we explore how effective leaders are the architects of success, guiding and inspiring their dream teams to achieve extraordinary results.

SIX

A – Accelerate Exceptional Leadership

I've spent countless hours in boardrooms, starting with my days as a young consultant. I've watched leaders navigate challenges and seize opportunities, and observed how some inspire, while others merely manage. It's the difference between building a house of cards and constructing a skyscraper. Leadership is about more than titles; it's about inspiring teams and building a lasting legacy through trust and impact. In today's dynamic and often-volatile business environment, we need leadership that goes beyond simply giving orders or chasing numbers. So let's dive deep into what it takes to be a truly exceptional leader in Africa: setting a clear vision, fostering trust, and empowering the next generation of leaders so we can build leaders who not only succeed but inspire others to do the same.

Driving leadership from the top

Leadership isn't just about titles; it's about action. It's about setting the tone, about leading by example. And, let's be honest, sometimes it's about tough love. For example, I once joined an organization that had a problem with discipline – particularly time discipline. I knew there was a problem when, as my first meeting approached, my assistant mentioned that she would start calling colleagues to remind them to join. I stopped her immediately, asking her whether or not we employ adults at this company. I entered the virtual meeting room five minutes before the start of the meeting and waited. The scheduled start of the meeting came and went. Five minutes later, I left the meeting room, asked my assistant to query the people as to why they missed our meeting, and went on about my day. Word quickly spread through the organization, and my local colleagues very soon appeared early to any meeting, even beating colleagues living in more traditionally time-conscious cultures. That's the reality of leadership. It's about making hard choices, setting expectations, and holding people accountable. It's about inspiring your team to be their best, even when the going gets tough. In this case, it was about teaching them that punctuality isn't just about respect for others; it's a reflection of our commitment to excellence.

Your leadership style sets the tone for your entire organization. Are you building a culture of fear or a culture of trust? Are you inspiring innovation or stifling creativity? The choice is yours. Remember, people watch what you do, not just what you say. Your actions as a leader have a cascading impact on your team, your customers, and even your community. It's about more than just hitting targets; it's about leaving a legacy.

Going beyond orders and numbers

Leadership isn't about bossing people around. It's about inspiring them to greatness. It's about creating an environment where everyone feels empowered to contribute and grow. It's about building trust, not fear. I joined another organization with one leader who was very much into ruling by fear. On one late Friday evening, as we were still all at the office, I could hear his team's music and laughter floating through the walls. I asked one of my colleagues why they weren't nervous about my still being there in the office to hear them, even though their boss wasn't around. I hope that I will never forget his response: "Would you rather have our fear or our respect?"

Sustainable leadership goes beyond the traditional command-and-control approach. Effective leaders are not afraid to ask questions and admit they don't have all the answers. Shifting from a know-it-all posture to an empowering and collaborative style fosters a culture where employees feel valued for their unique perspectives and encouraged to contribute their ideas.

However, communicating a clear vision is essential to sustainable leadership. A compelling vision provides a sense of purpose and direction for the organization, motivating employees to act. Leaders who coach their employees invest in their growth, creating a culture of continuous learning and equipping them with leadership skills for their own roles. Recognizing and celebrating leadership behaviors reinforces their importance and encourages others to step up.

Aligning leadership development with strategic goals

Leadership is also about execution, about turning your vision and lofty ideas into tangible results. Leadership development shouldn't be an afterthought; it's a strategic imperative. To ensure organizational initiatives align with your overall strategy, identify the leadership skills needed for success. Consider the core competencies and behaviors that will enable your leaders to achieve your strategic objectives, and design targeted programs that address specific needs at various stages of growth. For example, a young startup might prioritize innovation and risk-taking, while a more established company might focus on leadership for change management.

In one organization, I implemented a leadership development program with a specific focus on cultivating managers, targeted to address a critical need for the company's growth at that stage. This program equipped managers with the ability to translate the company's overarching vision into actionable plans for their individual teams. This meant taking big-picture goals and translating them into concrete steps that their teams could execute daily. If the company's vision was a large, intricate map, the strategic thinking program essentially gave managers the tools they needed to plan specific routes for their teams to follow, ensuring everyone was aligned and working toward the same objectives. The program was a game-changer for that company. It wasn't just about learning new skills; it was about transforming mindsets. It was about equipping leaders with the tools they needed to succeed. At the end aligning goals with leadership development is not just about training people; it's also about creating leaders who can drive your strategy forward.

Exceptional leadership in action

Let's talk about the business leaders who are shaping Africa's story. They aren't just CEOs; they're visionaries, innovators, and change-makers. They inspire us to dream bigger and aim higher. Think about Mo Ibrahim, for example, a Sudanese entrepreneur who didn't just build a telecommunications company into a pan-African giant but transformed an industry. He put people first, focused on quality, and built a legacy that's still inspiring entrepreneurs today. Consider Ibukun Awosika, the trailblazing former chair of First

Bank of Nigeria. A self-made entrepreneur, she not only navigated the complexities of the Nigerian banking sector but also used her platform to champion women's empowerment and social responsibility. Her visionary leadership transformed First Bank into a leading financial institution, setting a new standard for corporate governance and ethical business practices in Africa. Then there's James Mwangi's leadership at Equity Bank in Kenya. He didn't just create a bank out of a struggling building society; he created a financial revolution. He made banking accessible to millions, proving that profit and purpose can go hand-in-hand. We need more of this kind of leader: leaders who see beyond the bottom line. Leaders who are passionate about Africa's potential. Leaders who build a better future for us all. Let's learn from their examples and create our own legacy.

But a solid foundation is just the beginning. To truly unlock the potential of your organization, you need to build trust. This includes trust between leaders and employees, between colleagues, and across all levels of the company. This trust is the mortar that binds the bricks of leadership together, creating a space where collaboration, innovation, and mutual respect can flourish. In the next section, we'll explore how to cultivate this essential ingredient: trust.

Building trust in your organization

We've seen how a clear vision, empowered employees, and a commitment to ethical practices create a strong foundation for organizations. But just like a house needs more than a foundation to stand tall, a company needs trust to truly flourish. Trust between leaders and employees, between colleagues, and across all levels of the company is the mortar that binds the bricks of leadership together. It creates a space where collaboration, innovation, and mutual respect can take root and grow.

Imagine your organization as a team tasked with building a bridge. A strong leader sets the vision for the bridge, empowers each team member with their specific role, and ensures everyone has the tools they need. But if the team members don't trust each other – if the engineer doesn't trust the welder's skills or the architect doesn't trust the foreman's judgment – cracks will inevitably appear, jeopardizing the entire project. Trust is the invisible safety net that allows everyone to take risks, share ideas, and hold each other accountable for achieving the common goal. So how do we build this essential ingredient? Let's delve into two key strategies for fostering trust in your organization: encouraging transparency within your organization and building trust with those outside your organization.

Encouraging transparency as the cornerstone of trust

Transparency and safety are key elements of building trust. Employees need to feel comfortable speaking their minds and asking questions without fear of reprisal. This requires transparency from leadership. When leaders are open and honest about the company's direction, challenges, and decision-making processes, they foster a sense of security and psychological safety in employees. When leaders keep vital financial information close to the vest or make decisions behind closed doors, the lack of transparency breeds suspicion and distrust. On the other hand, regularly communicating company performance updates, even when the news isn't great, demonstrates a willingness to be truthful and accountable. This transparency builds trust and allows employees to feel invested in the company's success.

You play a pivotal role in fostering a culture of accountability and transparency in your organization. Remember that people watch what you do more than what you say. If you are secretive or avoid taking responsibility for your mistakes, you send a message that you do not value transparency and accountability. On the other hand, when you readily admit to mistakes, celebrate successes achieved through teamwork, and hold yourself accountable to the same standards you expect of others, you demonstrate genuine leadership.

Your authenticity builds trust and encourages a culture where everyone feels empowered to take ownership and hold themselves and their colleagues accountable for achieving results. *Transparency* isn't just a buzzword; it's the foundation of trust. It's about being open, honest, and accountable. It's about treating your team like partners, not just employees.

Building trust beyond your walls

Trust is the currency of business. It's what turns clients into partners, employees into advocates, and communities into supporters. It's not just about what you say; it's about what you do. Transparency again plays a key role here. Being transparent about your company's practices, social impact initiatives, and commitment to ethical sourcing builds trust with stakeholders. Fulfilling your promises and delivering on commitments strengthens this trust even further. Ethical leadership is also paramount to fostering a trustworthy environment. Leaders who set a high standard of integrity and make ethical decisions, even when it's difficult, inspire trust. And you must lead by example. Employees are more likely to trust and follow leaders who walk the walk, not just talk the talk.

Saying you value something is great, but backing it up with actions is even better. Imagine a company that publicly touts its commitment to sustainability but is caught engaging in environmentally harmful practices. This hypocrisy destroys trust not only with employees but also with customers, partners, and the community. On the other hand, a company that prioritizes ethical sourcing, fair labor practices, and environmental responsibility demonstrates its commitment to its values through its actions. This consistency between words and actions builds trust and fosters a positive reputation. If your company preaches diversity but has a leadership team that looks exactly alike, there's a gap between your words and deeds, and the inconsistency destroys trust. On the other hand, a company that actively promotes diversity in hiring, celebrates the contributions of all employees, and invests in unconscious bias training shows its commitment through concrete actions. This alignment between values and actions builds trust and strengthens the company culture.

Trust is the foundation of every strong relationship, whether it's with your employees, your customers, or your community. It's about being reliable, consistent, and authentic. Create a culture of trust in your organization, where everyone feels valued and respected, where people know they can count on you, and where your word is your bond.

Building trust: the payoff

Let's talk about the bottom line. Trust isn't just a feel-good factor; it's a business imperative. Trust is the invisible glue that holds everything together. It's the foundation of strong relationships, successful partnerships, and thriving businesses. When people trust you, they're more likely to take risks, collaborate, and go the extra mile.

Trust is especially important for us here in Africa, where formal systems might be less established. Strong corporate governance built on transparency, accountability, and ethical conduct fosters trust not only within the company but also with outsiders, like investors and banks. That trust is essential for getting funding and navigating the business environment. For example, a business owner who uses company money for personal things or cooks the books destroys trust with investors, making it nearly impossible to secure funding for future growth. However, a business owner that acts ethically, maintains clear financial records, and conducts business with integrity builds trust with stakeholders. That trust opens doors to new opportunities and positions the company for long-term success.

But trust is a continual process. You must earn it and keep it. That means being transparent, honest, and accountable. It means delivering on your promises, time and time again. It means building a reputation for reliability, consistency, and integrity. It means being a company that people can count on.

Rebuilding trust after a breach

Even the most trustworthy organizations can face challenges. Sometimes, mistakes are made or ethical lapses occur. I've seen businesses crumble because of a single breach of trust. It's a painful lesson, but it's a necessary one. When things go wrong, don't deny it or make excuses. Own up to it, learn from it, and make it right. The most important thing after a breach of trust is how you respond:

- **Acknowledge the mistake:** The first step is to admit the mistake or wrongdoing publicly and sincerely. Avoid downplaying the situation or making excuses.

- **Take responsibility:** The leadership team needs to be answerable for the situation. This demonstrates accountability and a commitment to doing better.

- **Communicate a clear plan:** Outline a distinct strategy for how you will address the issue and prevent it from happening again. Transparency is key here.

- **Demonstrate change:** Don't just talk the talk, walk the walk. Take concrete steps to implement the plan and show that you're serious about rebuilding trust.

Once, one of my employees decided to make a substantial payment to a customer without the approval of his manager, a significant enough mistake that would normally have led to his dismissal. However, his manager responded by acknowledging his team member's mistake and accepting the necessary responsibility, then communicating a clear plan to my leadership team to address the issue and, most importantly, took action to prevent similar situations from happening again. Through this process of transparency, accountability, and corrective action, both he and the team member who had actually erred were able to rebuild trust with me and the rest of the leadership team.

Remember, trust is earned, not given. It's a journey, not a destination. By following these strategies and learning from the experiences of others, you can foster an environment where trust thrives. This, in turn, will empower your employees, strengthen your relationships with stakeholders, and ultimately propel your venture to new heights. Remember, trust is the mortar that binds your organization, creating a foundation for collaboration, innovation, and long-term success. Invest in building trust and watch your business flourish. In the next section, we'll discuss how to lead an international team.

Leading across borders

Imagine your company stretches across the continent, a vibrant orchestra of talented individuals united by a shared vision but separated by lines on a map. How do you conduct this symphony of talent? The answer isn't to shout orders from a central HQ. It's to unleash the leadership potential within everyone while navigating different cultures, time zones, and work styles. This means fostering collaboration and building a global mindset – all without a single plane ticket.

Forget the larger-than-life CEO barking orders from the corner office. Leaders come in all shapes and sizes. They might be the quiet strategist who solves problems with a calm smile or the team player whose dedication inspires others. When searching for leaders on your team, look beyond titles and seek potential. Remember that titles don't tell the whole story. Recognize initiative, a passion for the work, and the ability to inspire – these are the hallmarks of a leader anywhere on the globe.

Cultural sensitivity is key, together with leadership assessment tools adapted for the diverse backgrounds that make up your global team. Look for individuals who've thrived in multicultural environments or possess strong intercultural communication skills. These "bridge builders" can excel in their roles and connect teams from various cultures. Remember, the world is getting smaller, but our challenges are getting bigger. We need leaders who can think globally and act locally. Let's create a new generation of leaders who are ready to shape the future of Africa and the world.

Empowering the middle

Middle managers are the unsung heroes of any organization. They're the bridge between the C-suite and the frontline. They're the ones who make things happen.

I've seen too many talented people get stuck in middle management. They have the potential to be great leaders, but they're often overlooked. It's time to change that. Empower them to become leaders, not just managers.

You can transform middle managers into leaders by investing in them. Give them the tools, training, and support they need to navigate the complexities of global leadership. Empower them to make decisions, solve problems, and inspire their teams. Rather than leaving them stranded, offer your ongoing support to address the challenges they face in their unique cultural contexts. Remember, a strong middle management team is the backbone of any successful organization. Build one that's ready to take on the world.

Maintaining consistent harmony

Leading a global team is akin to conducting an orchestra. Each musician brings their unique instrument, style, and interpretation. The conductor's role isn't to dictate every note, but to harmonize the ensemble, to create a whole that's greater than the sum of its parts. Cultural harmony isn't merely about acknowledging differences; it's about leveraging them for innovation. It's about creating an environment where everyone feels valued, respected, and empowered to contribute their unique perspective. To achieve this, you must be aware of different communication styles and adapt yours to avoid misunderstandings. What constitutes good leadership can differ according to culture. Some cultures expect top-down leadership, while others are more consensus-driven. Understanding these differences and adjusting your approach to fit the context will prevent frustration. Be flexible and willing to adapt your approach based on the cultural context.

I recall one project where we had a team made up of an Italian based in Morocco, an American based in Germany, a Swiss who floated easily around Africa, all directed by me, the Nigerian based in Kenya! As each of us were senior executives with such varied backgrounds, sometimes – many times – we struggled to find common ground. However, by continuously facilitating open dialogue, whether via conference calls or WhatsApp, and encouraging shared physical experiences whenever we happened to be in the same location, I transformed potential points of conflict into catalysts for creativity and productivity. This experience was a testament to the power of diversity when it's harnessed effectively.

Building a consistent leadership culture for a diverse workforce doesn't mean imposing a one-size-fits-all approach on everyone. While it's important to establish a core set of values that represents your company's overall mission, it's just as important to adapt your delivery to resonate with the diverse cultures represented on your team. Move beyond tolerance and embrace diversity. Create teams where differences are seen as strengths, not weaknesses, and you'll build a global community where everyone feels like they belong.

Leading as one team

Technology is undoubtedly our ally in this globalized world. It provides the infrastructure for seamless communication and collaboration. Video conferencing, project management tools, and real-time document sharing have revolutionized how teams operate across borders. But technology is just a tool; it's the human element that truly brings it to life, and for diverse teams, using the technology to its full potential depends on having a team equipped to work with people from a variety of cultures.

You can prepare your team for cultural diversity in a couple of ways. Invest in cultural competency training for your leadership team. This will help them to appreciate diverse perspectives and communication styles, leading to smoother collaboration. It's about cultivating a culture of trust, respect, and open communication. It's about creating a sense of psychological safety, where team members feel empowered to share their ideas, challenge the status quo, and learn from each other. It's about recognizing and valuing the diverse perspectives that each team member brings to the table. You can also assign projects for teams with members from different regions to work on together. Collaboration will foster shared purpose and understanding as the teams learn from each other's strengths.

Successful global teams don't just tolerate differences; they celebrate them. They find ways to leverage cultural nuances for innovation. They create an environment where everyone feels like they belong and can contribute meaningfully to the team's success. Remember, you're not just building a team; you're building a community. You're creating a global network of talent, connected by a shared purpose. Celebrating differences will help you harness the power of technology and the strength of human connection to build extraordinary teams that drive extraordinary results.

Seeing the big picture

Exceptional leadership doesn't happen by accident. It's not about having a title; it's about delivering results. It's about creating a positive impact, inspiring teams, and driving growth. But to know when you've got it, you need to be able to measure it. That means tracking not just the financial numbers, but the ones that matter: employee engagement, customer satisfaction, and innovation. This will show you how your leaders impact the metrics. Seeing the big picture means going beyond the traditional performance reviews. Get feedback from all angles – from the team, from peers, from customers. Create a culture of continuous feedback where everyone is learning and growing. Remember, leadership is a journey, not a destination. Measure your progress, celebrate your wins, and learn from your challenges. This will help you create a leadership culture that's not just about the top, but about empowering everyone to lead.

Final thoughts

The world these days is no longer limited to what's outside your office window; it's a vibrant orchestra of talent waiting to play a masterpiece. Forget the days of the lone conductor barking orders from a central stage. Leadership now transcends borders and titles. It requires recognizing the hidden melodies within every member of your team, fostering a collaborative spirit that celebrates diverse perspectives, and empowering everyone to contribute their unique voice to the symphony of success.

This symphony won't play itself, however. It requires *you* to become the conductor, the one who unlocks the potential within your team. By following these strategies, you won't simply build a global team. You'll cultivate a global orchestra where the quiet strategist from Uganda solves problems with a calm smile, the team player from Nigeria inspires with their passion and dedication, and the violinist from Namibia weaves melodies that resonate across continents. This is the power of leading people around the world: a powerful, diverse chorus playing a single, magnificent song.

And while this strong leadership is essential for a thriving organization, a robust governance framework provides the foundation for sustainable growth. As we delve into Chapter 7, we will explore the key principles of good governance and how to navigate the regulatory landscape.

SEVEN

L – Leverage Governance For Sustainable Growth

Congratulations! You've taken the plunge and launched your dream company, with the strategy, team, and leadership in place to build a thriving enterprise poised to make its mark. But before diving headfirst into the exciting world of business operations, let's take a moment to understand the regulatory landscape. Don't worry, I'll try not to make this a snoozefest of legalese. Rather, I'll translate the complexities into clear, actionable steps to ensure your business runs smoothly and stays compliant.

Navigating your regulatory landscape

Imagine regulations as the road map that guides your entrepreneurial journey across Africa. While the specifics might differ slightly from country to country, here's a general overview of some of the key regulatory areas you'll likely encounter:

- **Business registration as your official launch pad:** Every country has a process for registering businesses, typically involving specific government agencies. This process involves choosing a business structure (e.g., sole proprietorship, partnership, limited liability company [LLC]), selecting a catchy name, and obtaining necessary licenses and permits. Think of this as getting your driver's license for the business world.

- **Tax compliance to fuel national development:** As an entrepreneur, contributing your fair share to national development is crucial. Tax regulations define which taxes your business needs to pay (e.g., income tax, value-added tax, import duties), when you need to pay them, and how to file your tax returns. Remember, a good reputation as a tax-compliant business goes a long way toward establishing trust.

- **Labor laws to empower your workforce:** Your employees are the engine that drives your business forward. Labor laws ensure they're treated fairly, with regulations covering minimum wage, working hours, sick leave, and termination procedures. Following these laws fosters a positive work environment and a happy, productive team.

- **Environmental stewardship leading to a greener Africa:** Africa boasts breathtaking landscapes, and protecting them is a shared responsibility. Environmental regulations cover areas like waste management, pollution control, and sustainable resource utilization. By adhering to these regulations, you contribute to a greener Africa, which is good for not only people and the planet but also for your company's image.

- **Industry-specific rules tailored to your sector:** Depending on your industry, you might encounter additional regulations. For instance, a food processing company might need to comply with specific hygiene and safety standards, while a financial services firm would be subject to regulations regarding consumer protection and anti-money laundering measures. Think of these as specialized driving lanes for your specific industry.

Essential resources for your regulatory toolkit

Navigating this regulatory maze can be a daunting task, but it's a crucial step toward ensuring compliance and long-term success. It doesn't have to be a solo journey, however; there are a wealth of resources available to guide you:

- **Government websites:** Most governments offer comprehensive online platforms that outline business registration procedures, tax regulations, and labor laws. These websites are a great starting point for understanding the legal system within which your business operates.

- **Business registration agencies:** If you're unsure about the specific requirements for registering your business, consider seeking assistance from a business registration agency. These specialized agencies can provide expert guidance and help you navigate the registration process efficiently.

- **Industry associations:** Joining industry-specific associations can connect you with other business owners facing similar challenges. These associations often offer valuable insights into relevant regulations, best practices, and networking opportunities.

- **Legal and compliance experts:** For complex regulatory matters, it's advisable to seek professional advice from legal and compliance experts. They can provide tailored guidance, help you interpret regulations, and ensure that your business is in full compliance with the law.

Compliance as a growth catalyst

At this point, regulations might seem like hoops to jump through, but a shift in perspective can unlock hidden benefits. By understanding and adhering to regulations, you not only avoid legal pitfalls but also build the trust with stakeholders, customers, and partners that we discussed in Chapter 6. Moreover, regulations often reflect a country's economic priorities, providing valuable insights into market trends and potential opportunities. For example, I knew a Zambian entrepreneur who launched a revolutionary solar-powered irrigation system for smallholder farmers. By understanding and complying with renewable energy regulations, she not only ensured her business's legality but also gained access to government subsidies and tax breaks, propelling her agtech business to remarkable success.

Compliance isn't just a legal obligation; it's a strategic advantage. Here's how you can foster a culture of compliance within your organization, creating a solid foundation for sustainable growth:

- **Lead by example:** Demonstrate your commitment to compliance through your actions and communication.

- **Make compliance accessible:** Break down complex regulations into easily understandable terms.

- **Embed compliance in daily operations:** Integrate compliance into your routine processes.

- **Invest in training and awareness:** Keep your team informed about regulatory changes.

- **Foster open communication:** Encourage employees to raise compliance concerns.

- **Leverage technology:** Utilize technology to automate compliance tasks and streamline processes.

- **Celebrate successes:** Recognize and reward compliance achievements.

- **Empower compliance champions:** Identify and support employees who work toward compliance.

- **Seek expert guidance:** Consult with professionals for complex regulatory matters.

By embracing compliance as a strategic imperative, you're not just checking boxes but building a strong foundation for your business. Remember, in Africa's dynamic markets, a commitment to ethical and responsible business practices is not just a legal requirement; it's a competitive advantage that sets you apart and paves the way for a sustainable and impactful future. So embrace compliance – it's the secret weapon your business needs to thrive.

Regulations as allies, not obstacles

We've talked about navigating the regulatory maze in Africa, but here's the secret most people miss: regulations can be your allies, not just obstacles. Imagine regulations as signposts in a bustling marketplace, guiding you toward areas with high foot traffic and loyal customers. By understanding and strategically navigating regulations, you can unlock a treasure trove of opportunities for your venture. For example, I know a precision medicine company in West Africa that has gone through the long and onerous journey of not only obtaining all required local certificates but additionally becoming the only lab in the region with dual ISO accreditations in molecular diagnostics and biobanking. Because of these international certifications, the company has been able to land industry participants who bring expanded capabilities, opportunities, insights, market access, research opportunities, and enhanced access to innovative, high-quality diagnostics and personalized healthcare solutions. Additionally, it has secured multiple industry-sponsored clinical research services contracts worth over $1 million in revenue within a single year. Thanks to its commitment to meeting local and international regulations, the company can now focus on its vision of redefining healthcare and making precision medicine in Africa a reality.

Here are four ways you can transform regulations from a necessary chore into a springboard for growth:

1. **Gain a competitive edge by standing out from the crowd:** While regulations might initially seem like bureaucratic hurdles, you can transform them into strategic assets that help you stand out from the crowd in a competitive marketplace. Adhering to regulations can elevate your business from merely compliant to a standout in the marketplace. Think of compliance as a quality certification that signals to consumers your commitment to exacting standards and ethical practices. This trust-building can significantly enhance your brand reputation, attracting customers who value responsible businesses. Moreover, regulations can stimulate innovation. By viewing them as challenges to overcome, you can discover creative solutions that not only meet compliance standards but also improve your products or services. For instance, environmental regulations could inspire you to develop innovative energy-efficient production processes, providing a competitive edge and reducing your environmental impact.

2. **Unlock new markets using regulations as gateways:** Regulations can be your passport to new markets. Just as gatekeepers ensure only qualified vendors enter a lucrative trade fair, compliance can unlock opportunities for your business. By adhering to export regulations, for example, you gain access to a wider customer

base. Demonstrating a strong compliance culture can also increase your chances of securing government contracts. Moreover, understanding regional trade bloc initiatives like ECOWAS (Economic Community of West African States) and COMESA (Common Market for Eastern and Southern Africa) positions your business for future growth within the continent.

3. **Build trust with stakeholders as a foundation for growth:** Strong stakeholder relationships are the bedrock of any successful business. Compliance acts as the cement binding these relationships together. Just as a sturdy foundation supports a thriving market stall, adhering to regulations fosters trust among investors, partners, and customers. By operating transparently and ethically, you build a solid reputation that attracts and retains valuable stakeholders. Moreover, compliance protects your business from unfair competition, creating a level playing field where you can focus on growth and innovation. A commitment to compliance makes you a more reliable and trustworthy partner. This fosters long-term relationships with suppliers, distributors, and other stakeholders, creating a strong ecosystem that supports your business growth.

4. **Proactively engage and build relationships with regulatory bodies:** Rather than viewing regulatory bodies solely as rule enforcers, look

at them as potential allies in your business journey. By proactively engaging with them, you can gain valuable insights, build supportive relationships, and even help shape future regulations. Stay informed about upcoming changes, seek clarification when needed, and participate in public consultations. This collaborative approach will transform regulatory bodies from obstacles to partners in your growth strategy.

Adopting this Afro-optimist perspective and viewing regulations as allies will help you transform them from hurdles into stepping stones for growth. Remember, a strong compliance culture is not just about ticking boxes; it also unlocks a world of opportunities.

Building governance for growth

Africa's ambitious spirit is undeniable. Africa has witnessed the rise of passionate founders chasing bold dreams. Yet, challenges persist, and even the most promising ventures can falter due to mismanagement. The solution lies in strong corporate governance. Corporate governance is the cornerstone of sustainable business success. It's about building a foundation of trust, accountability, and ethical leadership, with trust as the most valuable currency in low-trust environments. While regulations provide the manual, governance is the engine that drives your business forward. It's your shield against uncertainty, a magnet for investors, and a catalyst for innovation.

Imagine a company where decisions are made with clarity and purpose, stakeholders trust the leaders, and growth aligns with societal impact. That's the power of governance. It's about more than just compliance; it's about shaping a legacy. Corporate governance is your personal roadmap to exceptional leadership. It equips you to lead with purpose, integrity, and a relentless commitment to progress. It's not just about the company you build; it's about the legacy you leave behind. Be the leader who not only rises but lifts others with you. As Africa takes its rightful place on the global stage, strong governance practices will define the leaders who shape our future. This journey is ours to embrace. It's a commitment to uphold and a vision to realize.

Demystifying governance structures

Now, let's delve deeper. The business world can be a labyrinth of guidance structures – boards of directors, advisory boards, and individual advisers. While all aim for success, their functions and compositions differ significantly, and each serves a distinct purpose:

- **Boards of directors (BoD) are the pillars of governance.** The BoD is the formal governing body, elected by shareholders, with legal responsibility for the company's direction. The

BoD sets strategy, appoints leadership, approves major decisions, and ensures ethical conduct. BoDs are typically made up of a mix of internal (senior executives) and external (independent experts) directors and have the ultimate decision-making authority.

- **Advisory boards are catalysts for strategic growth.** Composed only of external experts, advisory boards offer non-binding strategic advice, valuable insights, and fresh perspectives. They function as sounding boards for management on critical issues, identifying opportunities and challenges. Advisory boards often comprise specialists in finance, marketing, or legal matters. They may receive compensation (stock options, honorariums) but lack voting rights.

- **Board and CEO advisers provide personalized expertise.** Specialized consultants can offer tailored advice, often on specific challenges. They provide deep expertise, in-depth analysis, industry insights, and confidential mentoring. Advisers are not formally part of the board structure and are compensated based on contracts. Like advisory boards, they lack decision-making authority but offer invaluable guidance.

Your company's optimal governance structure depends on its development stage, size, and goals. Early-stage startups might lean toward advisory boards, while mature companies seeking investment may require a formal board.

Building a governance culture

Effective governance isn't just about structures and processes; it's about fostering a culture of accountability, transparency, and ethical leadership. A good governance culture is the lifeblood of your organization, influencing decision-making, stakeholder relationships, and overall performance. Imagine a company where everyone feels empowered to speak up, where mistakes are seen as opportunities for growth, and where ethical conduct is a top priority. This is the kind of culture that thrives on good governance. Here's how you can cultivate a strong governance culture:

- **Prioritize transparency:** Open communication is essential. Share information freely, be honest about challenges, and actively seek feedback from your team. This fosters trust and builds a sense of ownership among employees.

- **Ensure accountability:** Make sure that everyone understands their role and responsibilities within the organization. Celebrate achievements and address shortcomings transparently. This sends a clear message that everyone is accountable for their actions and that there are no shortcuts to success.

- **Embrace diversity and inclusion:** This is essential for a thriving governance culture. A diverse leadership team brings varied perspectives, leading to more informed decisions and innovative solutions. By creating an inclusive environment, you can tap into your team's full potential and foster a culture of collaboration and respect.

- **Invest in training:** Equip your team with the knowledge and skills they need to understand governance principles and their roles within the organization. This can include training on topics such as ethics, compliance, and risk management.

- **Demonstrate ethical leadership:** This sets the tone for the entire company. Establish a strong commitment to ethical conduct at all levels of the organization. This means leading by example, making ethical decisions, and holding others accountable for their actions.

By cultivating a robust governance culture, you will create a durable foundation for sustainable growth and success. A culture of accountability, transparency, and ethical leadership can enhance your organization's reputation, attract and retain top talent, and build trust with stakeholders.

In addition to the above list, to fully harness the potential of governance, businesses must also embrace technology. It's the digital compass that empowers and navigates complex, data-driven decision-making and ensures transparency. By using technology to harness the power of analytics, businesses can gain valuable insights into performance, identify trends, and predict future outcomes. Digital platforms facilitate seamless collaboration among board members, executives, and stakeholders. Remember, however, that safeguarding sensitive data is paramount, so make sure to invest in robust cybersecurity solutions to protect your business and its stakeholders. By integrating technology into governance practices, you can improve your decision-making efficiency, enhance transparency and accountability, mitigate risks, foster collaboration, and strengthen stakeholder trust.

Final thoughts

Strong governance is the cornerstone of sustainable business success in Africa. It's about building trust, attracting investment, and shaping a brighter future. By understanding the various governance structures, building a culture of compliance, and actively engaging in the regulatory landscape, you can position your business for long-term growth and impact. Remember, you're not just building a company; you're shaping Africa's entrepreneurial story.

Building on the foundation of good governance, we now embark on a critical phase of your journey: securing growth capital. In the next chapter, my esteemed strategic partners, Seun Oshunkoya and Matthew Nash from Westwood Investment Consultancy, will provide invaluable insights on navigating the world of capital and maximizing its impact on your business.

EIGHT

E – Expand Your Impact Via Growth Capital

Seun Oshunkoya and Matthew Nash, Westwood Investment Consultancy

O nce you've laid the groundwork for governance and compliance, the next crucial step is to scale your business through strategic growth. By understanding how to leverage growth capital, both financial and non-financial, you will accelerate your journey and maximize your impact. In this chapter, Seun Oshunkoya and Matthew Nash, my strategic partners at Westwood Investment Consultancy, will help you explore the world of growth capital and discuss how best to harness its power.

Introducing Westwood Investment Consultancy Services

We became Afro-optimists before we even knew the term existed. However, in almost twenty-five years of living, working, and investing in Africa, Afro-optimism has been our default setting, as it must be for anyone serious about the continent's development. It is why we continue to build here, and it is why we were so honored when Adeolu asked us to provide a modest contribution to this much-needed book, that we didn't hesitate for a second.

Our company, Westwood Investment Consultancy Services, is a corporate financial advisory firm much like the Africa-focused companies Adeolu has discussed in the previous chapters. Our team is blended and multi-disciplinary, each member bringing their individual skillsets, networks, and experience together to work toward our collective Afro-optimist goals. Over the last two plus decades, our focus has been helping African businesses achieve full, seamless and transparent access to local and global markets, investment products and opportunities so that they can do their part for a brighter African future. We've also worked to link investors with full and de-risked African markets, people, and opportunities, broadening Africa's global influence. We have contributed to the Afro-optimism movement – a movement that seeks to unleash African excellence by fusing ambition with resilience – both as direct market participants and advisers to African businesses of all stripes, making us uniquely positioned to help you expand your own company's impact.

Your business must have capital. Without capital, your African ambitions, ideas and dreams can go nowhere. Many people think money is sexy, but that finance is super-complicated. Both may be true at the margins, but we must concede, the truth is far more mundane – to get capital, you must know *who* you are, *what* capital is, *where* it is, and *how* to get it. We, in our own small way, are here to help you with that.

Structuring your business for growth

We'll start by helping you establish *who* you are by guiding you in structuring your business. By establishing clear organizational structures, implementing operational systems, and articulating strategic goals that align with long-term growth objectives, you can achieve significant growth. We'll also discuss managing talent and finances with growth capital in mind.

Organizational structure

Your business's mission, vision, and core values are the very DNA of your enterprise. Start by defining these often-overlooked elements, taking care to avoid descending into generic platitudes that you think people *want* to hear. Rather, these elements should resonate with both internal and external stakeholders, establishing a solid foundation for the company culture and guiding strategic decisions. Although it may seem hard to avoid sounding somewhat clichéd, keep in mind that these statements are fundamental to who you are as a business. They should serve as your north star, especially when you must navigate the challenges that will inevitably arise and call you to question your foundational principles. Success and failure often rest on fine judgment calls, and clearly articulating your core values will help you make the right decisions.

Operational systems

As sector-agnostic advisers and investors in fast-moving African frontier markets, over the last twenty years we have had front-row seats to the raw and rampant changes in how businesses here operate. To keep up, African business leaders must implement robust operational systems that streamline processes, enhance productivity, and maintain quality standards. This includes adopting modern technologies and software solutions that facilitate efficient workflow management, inventory control, and customer relationship management.

The evolution of operational systems in the African hotel sector offers a good example of the dramatic impact systems have on businesses' growth. Africans are renowned for our fast-sprinting prowess in athletics, and our markets are no different: they move fast! As a CEO or senior business leader in Africa, you must reckon with the speed at which our markets move and adapt your strategy accordingly. Over the past two decades, hotel industry software solutions have dramatically advanced, enhancing workflow management, inventory control, and customer relationship management (CRM). In the early 2000s, the initial property management systems (PMS) offered basic functions like reservations, check-in and check-out, and guest billing, with limited CRM features focused on guest history and basic marketing. These early technologies had a significant impact on hotel operations and profitability.

Between the mid-2000s and early 2010s, PMS solutions became more advanced, integrating with other hotel systems and offering better reporting tools. Sophisticated inventory control systems provided real-time updates and improved housekeeping, while CRM systems grew more prevalent, enabling better data analysis, personalized marketing, and loyalty program management. The shift to cloud-based systems during this period allowed for greater flexibility, scalability, and cost savings. During the 2010s, these software solutions further evolved, increasing their integration and mobility. Platforms began combining PMS, CRM, and central reservation systems (CRS), while mobile technology enabled development of apps for staff management, along with mobile check-in and check-out for guests. Advanced revenue management tools optimized room rates and inventory based on demand forecasting and market analysis. Additionally, software became increasingly focused on enhancing guest communication through integrated messaging and service request platforms. From the late 2010s to the mid-2020s, the rise of generative AI and automation led to comprehensive platforms that integrated PMS, CRM, inventory management, and more. AI and machine learning were used to enhance guest personalization, predictive analytics, and automated marketing campaigns. The internet of things (IoT), a system of internet-connected devices that allow data collection and exchange, enables smart room controls and energy management, while sustainability features like energy monitoring and waste reduction tracking reflect growing eco-conscious trends in the industry.

The evolution of software solutions in the hotel industry is a remarkable illustration of the importance of understanding and implementing robust operational systems. It reflects both the broad technological advancements and changing guest expectations that have become crucial for hotels to remain competitive, efficient, guest-focused and, ultimately, profitable. As this example shows, your operational systems really matter, regardless of your sector.

Strategic planning

As the saying goes, if you fail to plan, you plan to fail. It's essential for your enterprise to develop a comprehensive business plan that outlines both short- and long-term goals. This plan should include detailed market analysis, competitive landscape assessment, and a roadmap for scaling operations. Regularly revisiting and updating your plan will ensure your company aligns with evolving market conditions and business objectives. Note that this plan is an internal document, distinct from, for example, an investor memorandum, which is meant for external viewers. There are plenty of resources (including this one) available to assist entrepreneurs and business leaders in this regard, but here are five tips that we have found useful over the years in strategic planning for businesses:

1. Ensure your goals are SMART (see Chapter 4).

2. Engage with stakeholders – be they employees, customers, suppliers, or investors – to gather insights and ensure your strategic plan considers their needs and expectations.

3. Pay very close attention to resource allocation – be it human, financial or technological – to ensure that your company adequately supports strategic initiatives.

4. Take risk management seriously. Whether it is financial-, operational-, or market-related, having a risk management plan in place ensures business continuity when challenges inevitably arise.

5. Develop well-defined performance metrics and KPIs that you can use to measure progress

toward your goals. Regularly track and analyze these metrics to assess performance and make data-driven decisions.

So many of our businesses on the continent fail unnecessarily because they do not plan strategically. For example, we had a telecoms business during Nigeria's transition from military to civilian government between the late 1990s and early 2000s. Our business was awarded coveted and costly government infrastructure and operating licenses as part of the drive to open the private sector. We engaged and collaborated with established international technical partners to provide the Nigerian public with discounted international call rates, leveraging call cards from fixed landlines. The market was massive, and the business took off. Who knew Nigerians liked to talk so much – and that we cover all four corners of the earth?

However, fast-forward three years, and we were selling the business because we failed to adequately plan for foreseeable changes in the market. The Global System for Mobile Communications (GSM) technology was no secret; it was known to us and to the world, and we knew it would come to dominate the African communications sector. Yet, we failed to dimension the implications of this fact and plan strategically for its impact on our business. We were caught on our heels and couldn't adapt quickly enough, operating under the mistaken notion that we could improvise our way through the changes. We learned the hard way – but you don't have to!

Talent management

Although this book deals exhaustively with the subject of talent, we would be remiss not to touch on it as part of the *who* aspect of capital access. Attracting and retaining skilled talent is, of course, crucial for growth. To achieve this, African business leaders must implement effective recruitment strategies, provide continuous training and development opportunities, and foster a supportive and inclusive work environment. They must also encourage innovation and creativity among employees, which can help drive the business forward.

It all begins with ensuring that every employee understands the company's mission, vision, and goals. A leader who creates a clear vision and culture helps motivate and engage talent. Building a culture that adheres to your values will foster an environment where employees feel connected and motivated. As business leaders, we must demonstrate the values, work ethic, and behaviors we expect from our team. Leadership by example, which you should infuse at all levels, is a powerful tool for tone-setting in any organization. Showing genuine interest in team members' well-being and career development is important, and at times, an avuncular, or parental, approach to your interactions with team members can be amazingly effective. However, this ought to be balanced with your capacity to be decisive, lead firmly and strategically, and make tough decisions when necessary.

One aspect of talent management that is often missed in corporate and SME Africa is succession planning. No matter the size of your business, regularly assessing your team to identify potential future leaders and creating development plans to prepare them for higher roles is smart and ensures business continuity in the event of unexpected departures. Furthermore, your organization's agility and ability to withstand the vicissitudes, or changeability, of doing business are dependent on the evolution of your team members' skill sets. Upskilling, reskilling, and deliberately designing your organization's talent are necessities to maintaining your business advantage.

As ever in today's world, automated and cloud-based solutions, such as SaaS (software as a service) providers, are available and can make a real difference in assisting you to attract and retain talent. We have worked with an African startup at the forefront of this space that has built a platform to effectively manage the entire HR lifecycle of African organizations. We have also experienced the benefits of partnering with full-service HR companies that can assist in recruitment, training and development and that offer tailored solutions for building a people plan. Whether you use technology or human assistance, don't be afraid to reach out for expert help in attracting and retaining talent.

Financial management

Enterprises that intend to survive and thrive over the long term must embrace and maintain sound financial practice by establishing transparent accounting systems, managing cash flow effectively, and planning for investments and expenses. Regular financial audits and assessments help identify potential risks and areas for improvement. We have witnessed the power of such simple practices to unlock hitherto unknown and un-utilized value in our clients' businesses. In recent times, we have encouraged our corporate clients to understand what it really means to be "investment-ready." We don't necessarily mean readiness for foreign direct investment. Our local capital markets are deep and very liquid, and local business owners, even if aware of these markets' existence, have no idea how to access them. It is only those businesses with sound corporate and financial practices that stand a chance: good governance (regular board meetings, proper recording of meeting minutes, clear resolutions), competent and effective management teams, sound accounting practices, and regular financial audits. We never cease to find joy in watching a client tidy up their corporate and financial affairs and gain funding or credit as a direct result.

Fueling your expansion

In this section, we will move on to the *what* and *where* parts of accessing capital. Of course, securing funding is vital for scaling up and achieving long-term success, but it must be *adequate* and *appropriate* capital. Understanding the distinct types of investments and how to attract them is crucial for senior business leaders. It may seem self-serving, given our own business, but that doesn't make it any less true: when embarking on a capital-raising exercise, your first port-of-call ought to be a reputable financial adviser.

Understanding types of capital

Financial adviser notwithstanding, company CEOs and senior business leaders should familiarize themselves with the diverse types of capital (i.e., equity, debt, mezzanine). Each type has its benefits and drawbacks, and the choice depends on your business's needs and growth stage. Although concepts such as equity and debt are widely and generally understood by non-finance professionals, we believe delving a little into some details is helpful.

Equity refers to an ownership interest in the company. This ownership interest confers rights to the income generated by the company to the investor and, depending on what other aspects and privileges are included in the ownership interest, may also confer certain rights regarding the operation of the business. A key question in raising equity capital is what percentage of the business the investor will be entitled to for their investment. Valuing equity can be complex, especially given the various stages of a company's lifecycle. We strongly urge you to consult with reputable financial advisers when seeking to understand how best to value your business. This subject matter is too vast and multifarious to be covered in detail in this chapter.

Debt financing involves borrowing funds that must be repaid within an agreed period, including both the principal and interest. The repayment can be structured in two ways: *amortizing* or *bullet*. In an amortizing loan, the principal is gradually paid down over the loan's tenure through equal payments, each including portions of interest and principal. In contrast, a bullet loan requires no principal repayment during the loan term; instead, the entire principal, along with accumulated interest, is paid in a single lump sum at the end of the loan period. Bullet payments are common in interest-only loans, where the borrower only pays interest throughout the loan term, with the full principal due at maturity.

Credit support plays a crucial role in debt financing, although many business leaders may be unaware of its significance. Credit support involves a third party that provides guarantees or insurance for loan repayment. In Africa, various agencies offer these guarantees to support specific transactions, such as loans to SMEs or for infrastructure projects. These agencies have substantial dollar balance sheets that enable them to provide necessary credit guarantees, which often influence the overall cost of capital. Additionally, firms offering credit insurance provide sureties, or formal guarantees, for loan repayments. While credit support comes at a cost, usually a percentage of the guaranteed amount, it is valuable when the guarantor's credit strength is superior to the borrower's. Through careful negotiation, the borrower may leverage credit support to save on interest rates. When seeking debt finance, you should be aware of the interest rates you might encounter. Several risk factors influence these rates, including company-, industry-, and country-specific risks. The base rate for interest should consider the interest rate at which the borrower's country borrows in international markets, with the actual rate rising based on the perceived risks.

Mezzanine finance is a hybrid form of financing that combines elements of both debt and equity. It is typically used to fund expansions, acquisitions, or significant investments when traditional bank loans are insufficient or unavailable. Mezzanine financing offers higher returns to investors than other types of debt, but with increased risk. It occupies a middle ground between debt and equity in terms of the lender's priority rights to income. In bankruptcy, debt providers are repaid first, followed by mezzanine lenders, and equity investors usually receive little or nothing. Mezzanine lenders, therefore, require returns that fall between those expected from debt and equity investments. This financing option often offers flexible repayment terms, such as interest-only payments for a period, with principal repayment deferred until the loan term ends.

Mezzanine financing has distinct advantages over equity financing. It is less likely to dilute, or decrease the value of, existing shareholders' shares, offers flexible terms tailored to cash flow and business needs, and allows companies to retain control, as mezzanine lenders typically do not require board seats or operational influence. Mezzanine financing also acts as a bridge between higher-priority debt and equity, enabling companies to finance growth without issuing new equity immediately. However, its high cost and complexity require careful consideration to ensure it aligns with your company's long-term goals and financial health.

Preparing for investment

We have now reached the *how* part of the capital-raising journey. Closing successfully on an investment requires serious preparation and copious tenacity. This brings to mind the aphorism, commonly attributed to Napoleon Bonaparte, "Victory belongs to the most persevering." This mindset is never more appropriate than for entrepreneurs looking to grow and scale their businesses through finance. As a CEO or senior business leader, you must develop compelling offering documentation (e.g., investor memorandum, teaser deck, pitch deck) that clearly outlines your business model, market potential, and growth strategy, highlighting also your unique value proposition, financial projections, and the potential return on investment.

Once you've established the underlying strength of your opportunity for investors, your next-most important criterion to ensure you successfully raise your capital is to ensure the quality of your offering documentation. Investors will make an initial assessment about the strength of your management team and the potential investment based on the quality of your documentation. In many cases, investors will reject even strong opportunities if the documentation is poorly prepared. Money managers are inundated with investment requests, so the quality and professionalism of the documentation becomes a straightforward way to filter out potentially bad investments. If your documentation is replete with typos, doesn't convey the essence of the opportunity, or fails to answer obvious questions that any prudent investor would ask, your deal will quickly be thrown into the dustbin.

At the beginning of a capital-raising exercise, you and your financial adviser may have an initial idea of the form the transaction will take. However, once distribution begins and interactions with investors are underway, you will invariably find that they have a different view of the transaction. By remaining open to change, you can align the transaction structure with market feedback and increase your chances of success. Additionally, remaining open and flexible can help you identify opportunities that weren't apparent initially.

Building and managing investor relationships

Building strong relationships with potential investors is crucial for any CEO or business owner. The process begins with researching and approaching investors who align with your business values and goals. Although we don't cover this topic here in detail, senior business leaders should also take time to learn about types of investors or lenders, including angel investors, venture capitalists, private equity firms, development finance institutions (DFI), family offices, sovereign wealth funds, crowdfunding, and government grants. It's essential to engage in transparent and open communication and be prepared to negotiate terms that are beneficial to both parties. Importantly, start building these relationships well before you need funding. Attending industry events, joining relevant networks, and leveraging connections are effective ways to meet potential investors.

Through years of experience as corporate financial advisers, we have observed a common tendency among promoters, senior business leaders, and CEOs to be overly selective about investors and avoid those they perceive as difficult. While it is natural to want to minimize effort, especially since courting each potential investor requires considerable work, it is crucial to remember that a deal is not done until the transaction is funded. The more potential investors you engage with, the more valuable your opportunity seems, as the fear of missing out (FOMO) can drive interest. Therefore, it is advisable to keep discussions open with all viable funders who express interest. Engaging with difficult investors should be viewed as an opportunity to refine your pitch and prepare for meetings with more enthusiastic investors. Remember, in the process of raising capital, you are essentially a salesperson – selling your ideas, your company's prospects, your vision, and your team's ability to execute on these promises.

Momentum is key to successfully closing a transaction. Once an investor expresses interest, it is vital to maintain this momentum to ensure the investor remains engaged. Investors are constantly being presented with new opportunities, so keeping their excitement alive is crucial. If you slow down or delay the process, there is a risk that the investor may move on to the next deal. Timing is critical, and things can change quickly, so it is important to keep the process moving forward.

When embarking on a capital-raising journey, you should also be prepared for the long haul. Rejections are a normal part of the process and should be expected. However, accepting the first "no" without persistence could lead to missed opportunities. You should approach each encounter with an investor as a learning opportunity where you can improve and refine your approach. *Deal fatigue*, where companies become tired of responding to prospects, is a real phenomenon, and it can cause you to miss out on potential funding. By starting the process with a marathon mindset, you can better weather challenges and stay focused on crossing the finish line.

Once you have secured your capital, it is crucial to stick to the plan you presented to investors. This builds trust and positions you well for future funding rounds.

Regular communication with your investors is also important, keeping them updated on the business's progress, challenges, and successes. This ongoing engagement not only maintains strong relationships but also ensures that your investors remain confident in your company's direction.

Expanding your reach

Having secured the requisite capital and structured your business for growth, the next hurdle is to translate these assets into tangible impact. This necessitates a strategic approach that encompasses people, partnerships, and a pan-African presence. There are no shortcuts to this, and gimmicks won't work. We have seen investors and business owners fail in their expansion ambitions by only paying lip-service to the need for tangible impact while pursuing profit over everything.

Africa's diverse cultural landscape presents both challenges and opportunities. A deep understanding of local customs, traditions, and business etiquette is paramount. By tailoring business practices to resonate with local sensibilities, you foster trust and cooperation, which are essential ingredients for sustainable growth. In our travels across the region over the last twenty years, we have found that effective cross-cultural communication is key to bridging cultural gaps. We have spent time engaging with community elders and local leaders, especially when bringing in foreign direct investors whose knowledge of the region is limited. Encouraging open dialogue within your organization and with external stakeholders, while also providing cultural competency training, can bridge divides and create a harmonious business environment. Flexibility and adaptability are key to navigating these cultural nuances. By aligning your business strategy with local demands and customs, you demonstrate respect and increase your chances of success. Furthermore, inclusive leadership, characterized by diversity at all levels, can foster innovation and ensure your business is responsive to the needs of your market.

Strategic networking is another cornerstone of expansion. Building and nurturing relationships with industry peers, potential partners, investors, and government officials can unlock new opportunities and provide invaluable support. Over the years, we have witnessed the power that networking events celebrating cultural festivities can have. Whether they observe religious events, such as Eid or Diwali, or local traditional events, such as the New Yam Festival, organizations that are cognizant of cultural festivals stand to gain a robust and sustainable footing across African markets. We have also actively encouraged corporate clients looking to scale across the region to sponsor local charities in a genuine bid to contribute directly to communities and ensure communities feel the organization's impact beyond its core business. Leveraging social media platforms can, of course, amplify your reach and facilitate connections with a wider audience. Collaborative initiatives such as joint ventures and partnerships can pool resources, expand market share, and mitigate risks. On-the-ground intelligence is as powerful as the multiplying effect of the internet. African markets, as we've mentioned, are fast-moving, and real-time capability to adapt to changing conditions puts your business ahead of the competition.

To maximize your impact, consider expanding your operations beyond national borders. A pan-African approach can unlock new markets, diversify revenue streams, and enhance your brand's reputation. However, cross-border expansion requires careful planning and execution. Thorough market research is essential to identify opportunities and potential challenges. Developing a robust entry strategy – including considerations for local regulations, cultural nuances, and competitive landscapes – is crucial. Building strong local partnerships can accelerate market penetration and provide invaluable insights. Moreover, effectively managing cross-cultural teams is essential for success. By fostering a culture of inclusivity and respect, you can harness the diverse talents of your workforce.

Final thoughts

The journey to expansion is undoubtedly fraught with challenges. Cultural misunderstandings, regulatory complexities, and competitive pressures can all pose significant hurdles. Yet, these are not insurmountable obstacles. They are opportunities to innovate, adapt, and learn. By embracing the spirit of Afro-optimism, we can harness the continent's potential and transform these challenges into stepping stones to success.

Remember, scaling your business is not just about growth; it's also about impact. It's about creating jobs, empowering communities, and contributing to Africa's economic development. The SCALE framework provides a robust roadmap for African businesses seeking to expand their impact:

- **Strategize your vision:** Develop a clear roadmap for growth, align your business with market needs, and leverage data-driven insights to inform decision-making.

- **Champion excellence:** Build a high-performing team with diverse perspectives and skills, fostering a culture of innovation and collaboration.

- **Accelerate exceptional leadership:** Inspire and empower your team, create a positive work environment, and develop future leaders.

- **Leverage governance for sustainable growth:** Establish strong governance practices, prioritize ESG factors, and build strategic partnerships.

- **Expand your impact via growth capital:** Secure the right funding, build strong investor relationships, and effectively utilize capital for growth.

By strategically planning ahead, cultivating a high-performance culture, developing exceptional leadership, leveraging robust governance, and effectively executing growth strategies, you can navigate the complexities of the African market, build resilient businesses, and become a catalyst for positive change. Embracing the SCALE framework, and fostering a culture of collaboration, innovation, and resilience, can help African businesses overcome challenges, seize opportunities, and become global leaders. The future of Africa is bright, and with the right leadership and strategies, you can play a pivotal role in shaping it.

With your new, fuller understanding of the SCALE framework, you can again complete the scorecard at https://zerconsulting.com/scaleyourbusiness to evaluate where you currently fall on the SCALE and leverage the guidelines we've provided here to close your confirmed gaps.

PART THREE
COLLABORATING FOR GLOBAL IMPACT

NINE
Thriving In Uncertain Times

As I stated right at the beginning of this book, I have always been ambitious. I was a straight-A student without being a nerd but preferred hanging out with the nerds anyway. I dominated in my chosen sports of basketball and track. I excelled in band, my chosen additional extracurricular. I was going places. So it was normal, when I left the safe world of academia to finally begin my career, that I set CEO as my target position. After all, a type-A personality like me would always aim for the "best," the "highest," the "grade-A" role. However, it wasn't very long into my career, perhaps already in that first year, before I realized that there was much more to life than getting good grades. Could life even be graded? As I watched the sacrifices the senior women around me had made to get to where they were,

I wondered if the sacrifice was too much. After all, I wanted marriage, I wanted kids (one girl and one boy), I wanted to be happy – I wanted it all, long before I knew that was a thing.

So I pivoted, thinking, "Well, let someone else take that number one spot. Let someone else make that sacrifice. Let someone else get their face on all the posters. I'd be happy just to set up a subsidiary office of the company I work for in my home country of Nigeria." But to do that, I had to get the heck out of the USA, at a time when that company wasn't super international. Thankfully, around this time, the company started actively encouraging international moves and internally advertising these positions, so I raised my hand for everything. A spot opened up in Mexico? Cool. I spoke Spanish fluently, so that seemed a natural one. Another in Brazil? Well, Portuguese couldn't be so far from Spanish, could it? How about dreary, rainy London instead? Sure, where does this sun-child sign up? That didn't work out; what about Zurich? And I was on the next plane to the interview.

I didn't get chosen for any of those jobs, but I did attract the notice of my bosses, who realized how keen I was on international life. So when a project in need of junior support came in from Europe, they came knocking on my door and asked whether I'd take on two clients: The Bank for International Settlements (BIS) and the EIB. My eager "yes" jumpstarted my international career. Sure, I was based in the same local location of Chicago,

USA, but I started building connections with two colleagues who would later become my bosses when my company finally formed an international team. When one of these colleagues moved back to Chicago from the UK to lead this team, I was one of the first folks he called on board. And when the other colleague was looking to expand the Europe-based side of this same international team, he called me, as well. *That's* how I finally made the physical move that finally got me out of the USA and into the same time zone as Africa.

But the coincidences didn't stop there. A few years later, I stood at a crossroads, having left my company of eleven years post-merger, trying to figure out the next step toward getting back to Nigeria. Then a former client reached out, asking whether I was interested in supporting them internally with the same project I had been driving externally as their consultant. Although it meant returning to Germany from where I was enjoying myself on the beaches of southern Turkey, I jumped at the opportunity to transition from giving advice to implementing it on the other side. However, when I went through the formal recruitment process, you can imagine my shock when I was screened out by their HR team. Thankfully, through that internal connection, I was able to reach out to the hiring manager directly to find out why he'd asked me to apply just to reject me shortly afterward. Long story short, that initial rejection turned into a formal offer within a few months, and shortly thereafter, I started another eleven-year career at a different global multinational.

I won't bore you with how, once I entered this new company, a seemingly random series of coffees and lunches led to one of the global heads of the organization approaching me to support him in driving a global transformation program. I also won't bore you with the story of how we later brought this initiative to Turkey, leading to another lunch with another CEO, who, upon finding out that my now-husband was Turkish, immediately encouraged me to join the effort in Turkey. I'll even skip the story of how my persistence about Africa within a company that had already pivoted *away* from Africa led to a meeting with a former McKinsey consultant who would later become the company's regional CEO for Africa. That CEO hired me to drive the company's acquisition strategy across the continent, simply because another former consultant from McKinsey, who happened to be part of my project team during a leadership development course, vouched for my abilities to lead huge initiatives. But I will slow down to tell you about the fateful text I received one Friday night in June 2020, when the same regional CEO, who was now my boss, wrote to me, "Can we talk?" I came out of that conversation in disbelief, having hardly heard a word he'd said after the first five: "We need you in Nigeria." And that's how I became a CEO.

Leadership lessons from the trenches

As I've mentioned, being a CEO isn't always glamorous. Forget the corner office with a skyline view; I took over my new Lagos-based role while stuck in Nairobi during the thick of the COVID-19 crisis, and my view was a sea of worried faces on my computer screen. Stepping in as the CEO of the subsidiary of a global multinational – a subsidiary I had helped acquire only a couple of years earlier – the pressure was immense. We were staring down the barrel of a pandemic-induced global economic meltdown, and our mothership was still insistent on realizing the growth and profits that had been promised them on paper.

This wasn't some textbook case study; this was real life, African life, Nigerian life, with all its complexities. We couldn't simply copy-and-paste solutions from Europe. But hey, that's the beauty of being an African entrepreneur, right? We've got hustle in our blood, an understanding of our communities, and an unshakable Afro-optimism that gets us through the toughest times. So how did we – a team of passionate Nigerians leading an international company – stop the bleeding during COVID? Here are a few hard-won lessons from the trenches, African style.

Lesson 1: Embrace empathy, even as you focus on the bottom line

Leading through a crisis is a brutal balancing act. During COVID, we faced a harsh reality: to ensure the company's survival, we had to make some tough decisions. One of the most difficult was implementing a redundancy program. Letting go of good people is never easy. But here's the thing: true empathy isn't about guaranteeing employment. It's also about taking responsibility for the long-term health of the company, which ultimately benefits all stakeholders, including our employees.

Here's how we approached this delicate situation with empathy at the forefront. First, transparency was key. We communicated openly and honestly with our team about the financial challenges we faced. We explored the rationale behind the redundancies, making sure it wasn't a knee-jerk reaction but a strategic move to secure a stronger future for the remaining employees. Second, we didn't just cut and run. We offered a generous severance package, outplacement services, and even partnered with local businesses to offer potential job opportunities for those leaving. It wasn't a perfect solution, but it showed our departing colleagues that we valued their contributions and cared about their well-being. Finally, we prioritized reskilling and upskilling for the remaining team. We invested in training programs to ensure they had the skills needed to navigate the "new normal" of the post-COVID world. This not only improved their employability but also demonstrated our commitment to their growth, boosting morale within the company.

This experience taught me a valuable lesson: empathy doesn't mean shying away from difficult decisions. It means making those decisions with the well-being of your entire team – those staying and those leaving – in mind. It means being honest, offering support, and investing in the future, even when the present is bleak. Because the most compassionate act is ensuring the long-term survival of the company that provides a livelihood for so many. After all, a healthy company with a strong foundation is better positioned to support its employees and offer new opportunities down the line.

Lesson 2: Go beyond hustle to build a strategy for profitable growth

We've all heard stories of African hustle – our ability to get things done, no matter the obstacles. It's a powerful force, but during COVID, we learned that hustle alone doesn't guarantee success. We needed a new strategy – one focused on profitable growth, not just blind expansion. This was where we had to challenge conventional wisdom. Local competitors often chased after any client with a pulse, even if those clients were high-maintenance and drained their resources. We took a different approach. We conducted a ruthless audit of our client base, identifying those who weren't a good fit for our new, streamlined model. It wasn't an easy decision – some were big names, but they were also major drains on our profitability. Letting them go was a difficult pill to swallow, but it freed up resources for more strategic ventures. Our strategy wasn't about abandoning local excellence, but rather redefining it.

We embraced global best practices in risk management and claims processing, ensuring our products were top-notch. However, we delivered them through innovative, locally relevant channels like mobile apps and partnerships with local microfinance institutions. This blend of global quality and local accessibility became our sweet spot.

Here's the result: We attracted new clients who valued our commitment to both excellence and affordability. We streamlined our operations, becoming more efficient and profitable. Most importantly, we sent a clear message that our company stood for global standards delivered with a local touch. This experience taught me a powerful lesson: true growth isn't just about chasing numbers. It's about building a sustainable business model that delivers value to all stakeholders. Don't be afraid to break away from the pack, even if it means letting go of some big fish. Focus on building a strategy that prioritizes profitable growth, and you'll attract the right clients, who value a company that stands for global excellence within the local market.

Lesson 3: Grow your tribe via empowerment, flexibility, and recognition

Leading through a crisis is about more than just tough decisions; it's about building a team that can weather any storm. During COVID, I knew that to survive, we needed to transform the company into a truly empowering workplace. This meant not just fostering open communication and celebrating wins, but also implementing innovative HR practices that put our employees first. One of our biggest bets was formalizing a flexible work-from-anywhere policy for all employees, against the directive from our management to return to the office. For us, this wasn't just a trendy perk; it was a recognition of the realities of the modern Nigerian workforce, where many juggle family commitments and long commutes. By offering this flexibility, we empowered our team to achieve a healthy work-life balance, ultimately leading to increased productivity and morale. This focus on employee well-being didn't stop there. We invested heavily in training and development programs, ensuring our team had the skills needed to thrive in the post-COVID world. We also prioritized mental health support, recognizing the immense stress the pandemic placed on everyone.

These efforts didn't go unnoticed. In 2022, our company was proudly recognized with the Chartered Institute of Personnel Management of Nigeria's (CIPM) *HR Best Practice Awards*. This prestigious award wasn't just a validation of our efforts; it also elevated our company's reputation as an employer-of-choice. Top talent across Nigeria now saw our company as a place where they could not only grow professionally but also feel valued and supported. This experience taught me an enduring lesson: Building a dedicated team isn't about empty motivational speeches. It's about empowering employees, offering flexibility, and investing in their well-being. By prioritizing these elements, you can create a work environment that attracts and retains top talent, ultimately propelling your company toward success. Remember, a happy and empowered team is a powerful force, especially when navigating the uncharted waters of a crisis. And who knows? Your innovative HR practices might just land you an award or two, solidifying your company's reputation as a leader in its field.

The takeaway: Afro-optimism in action

We've covered a lot in this book, from crafting your strategy and building a team focused on delivering excellence to leveraging leadership, good governance, and the right capital to expand your reach. But let's remember, the journey won't always be smooth sailing. There will be challenges, moments when you want to give up. But that's where Afro-optimism kicks in. We Africans have a unique resilience, a creativity that knows no bounds, and an unwavering belief in a better future. These are the qualities that set us apart. Here are a few of the Afro-optimist strategies that I've picked up along the way:

- **Empathy is your superpower:** Even when making tough decisions, remember to put yourself in others' shoes. Understanding the needs of your stakeholders, from worried customers to departing employees, will help you make choices that benefit everyone overall.

- **Hustle with strategy:** We Africans are known for our hustle, but sometimes, blind ambition can lead us astray. Develop a clear strategy focused on profitable growth, prioritizing value over volume.

- **Build your tribe:** Your team is your greatest asset. Empower them, offer flexibility, and invest in their well-being. A happy and productive team is a winning team.

Remember, the road ahead won't be easy. There will be bumps and obstacles. But with Afro-optimism, strategic thinking, and a commitment to your team, you can not only weather the storm but emerge stronger than ever.

Plan B: The unexpected savior

Speaking of storms, "Always have a Plan B," is a business gospel I've preached for years. Yet, ironically, that very gospel once almost got me fired. It was during a particularly challenging time when I was leading a global transformation program. As one does, I decided it was time to discuss adequate compensation for my hard work and dedication. However, my request for a raise was denied. Rather than dwelling on the disappointment, I simply shrugged and said, "Well, there's always Plan B." What I meant was that I believed in the power of adaptability and the ability to find unexpected opportunities in the face of adversity. Apparently, my boss interpreted my comment as a veiled threat, and things got a little tense – until I quickly resolved the misunderstanding and conveyed to him what exactly I meant by this seemingly off-hand comment.

That incident helped me to crystalize into words what had been until then just a natural part of my thinking process: Plan B isn't just about having a backup plan; it's about cultivating the agility and foresight to identify and seize hidden opportunities within every crisis. In Africa, we're well-versed in navigating stormy waters. But even the best-laid plans can be swept away by unforeseen currents. That's when Plan B becomes your secret weapon. So how do we, the ambitious hustlers of Africa, turn these hidden opportunities into stepping stones for success? Let's dive in.

Your crisis survival kit

Crises are like sneaky pirates, leaving behind a mess of anxieties. But they also often bury a treasure chest of hidden opportunities. The key is to develop a sixth sense for sniffing out these hidden diamonds, and that's where your team comes in. Remember, your team is your greatest asset. When the going gets tough, gather your champions for a brainstorming session that will blow your mind. Challenge the status quo, encourage crazy ideas that might spark a breakthrough, and figure out how to repurpose what you already have. Think of it as using your company's toolbox to build something entirely new.

Once you've unearthed those hidden opportunities, it's time to get them sparkling. Here's your crisis survival kit, packed with practical steps to turn your Plan Bs into realities:

- **Reassess, adapt, and repeat:** Don't be afraid to take a long, hard look at your business model. Is what you're offering still relevant in this new landscape? Can you tweak it to fit the changing needs of the market? Remember, agility is key. Be prepared to adapt and iterate on your ideas as you go.

- **Communicate with clarity and empathy:** Crises can make everyone feel anxious and a little lost. That's why clear communication is crucial. Be open and honest with your team, your customers, and your stakeholders. Explain the challenges you're facing, the potential Plan Bs you're exploring, and how their contributions are vital for your success.

- **Embrace Afro-optimism:** Remember that Plan B comment that almost got me fired? Looking back, it was a lesson in miscommunication but also a reminder that sometimes the best opportunities are hidden in plain sight. We just need to be open enough to see them.

Plan B in action

M-KOPA

M-KOPA, a Kenyan-based solar energy company, is a prime example of a business that successfully implemented a Plan B strategy to address a significant challenge in the African market. Initially, M-KOPA focused on providing solar-powered home systems to customers in Kenya and other African countries. However, the company faced challenges such as the high upfront cost of solar systems. In response, M-KOPA implemented a pay-as-you-go (PAYG) model, allowing customers to purchase solar systems in installments using their mobile phones. This innovative approach made solar energy more accessible to low-income households and helped M-KOPA to overcome the challenge of upfront costs. By implementing a Plan B strategy and adapting to the challenges of the African market, M-KOPA has become a leading provider of solar energy in the region. The company's success has not only helped to improve the lives of millions of people but has also created new business opportunities and spurred innovation in the renewable energy sector.

Fawry

Fawry is an Egyptian fintech company that has successfully navigated challenges and implemented a Plan B strategy to become a leading player in the Egyptian market. Initially, Fawry focused on providing bill-payment services. However, the company faced challenges such as limited internet penetration and a lack of trust in digital payments among many Egyptians. In response, Fawry partnered with local retailers and agents to make its services more accessible to customers who either didn't have access to or were not comfortable using online channels. As it built trust, Fawry expanded its services to include mobile money transfers, airtime top-ups, and other financial services. By implementing a Plan B strategy and adapting to the challenges of the Egyptian market, Fawry became a leading fintech company in the region. The company's success has not only helped to promote financial inclusion in Egypt but also created new business opportunities and spurred innovation in the fintech sector.

Jumia

Jumia, the largest e-commerce platform in Africa, faced numerous challenges during its early years, including limited internet penetration, logistical difficulties, and skepticism about online shopping. To overcome these challenges, Jumia implemented several Plan B strategies, such as partnering with local logistics companies to improve its delivery services and reach customers in remote areas. Additionally, to address concerns about online payment security, Jumia introduced a cash-on-delivery option, allowing customers to pay for their orders upon receipt. It also expanded its product offerings beyond electronics and consumer goods to include groceries, fashion, and other categories. Finally, Jumia invested heavily in technology to improve its website and mobile app, making it easier for customers to shop online. By implementing these Plan B strategies, Jumia was able to overcome the challenges it faced and become a leading e-commerce platform in Africa. The company's success has helped to drive economic growth and create jobs in the region.

Resilience is the root of all Plan Bs

The entrepreneurial journey in Africa, like in any other region, is rarely a smooth ride. Setbacks are inevitable, but they can also be powerful catalysts for growth. Think of the bamboo tree: it spends years seemingly dormant, only to shoot up rapidly once its roots are firmly established. Similarly, business setbacks can strengthen our foundations and prepare us for future challenges. When faced with adversity, it's crucial to shift our perspective and view setbacks as opportunities for learning and growth. By analyzing our failures without self-blame, we can identify underlying issues and improve our strategies.

Resilience benefits from several important practices. Open communication through honest dialogue with your team, investors, and customers fosters trust and unity. Seeking support from mentors or peers can provide valuable insights and encouragement. Understanding cultural nuances is equally important. Different cultures have varying views on failure, and adapting your approach accordingly can enhance your organization's resilience. Finally, innovation is key to overcoming challenges. Africa's rich history of ingenuity can be your greatest asset. Embracing creativity and seeking innovative solutions can transform setbacks into stepping stones toward success.

Remember, the entrepreneurial journey is a marathon, not a sprint. By embracing challenges, learning from our mistakes, and seeking support, we can build the resilience needed to overcome any obstacle and achieve our goals. As Nelson Mandela wisely said, "The greatest glory of living lies not in never falling but in rising every time you fall" (Bennet, 1998).

Final thoughts

My journey as a CEO has taught me invaluable lessons about leadership, resilience, and the power of Plan B. From navigating unexpected career paths to leading through crises, I've learned that adaptability, foresight, and a positive outlook are essential for success. Africa is a continent full of opportunities, and with the right mindset and strategies, you can be a part of its success story. As I've learned, embracing the power of Plan B can lead to unexpected and rewarding outcomes. What's your own Plan B?

TEN

Partnering for a Thriving Africa

You've poured your blood, sweat, and tears into building your business in Africa. You've witnessed firsthand the challenges our communities face – from inadequate infrastructure to limited opportunities – pivoting to your Plans B, C, and D with alacrity. Your desire to succeed and make a difference has been unwavering, impressing both partners and investors alike. Now it's time to take your impact to the next level. The SCALE framework has provided a solid foundation, but to truly unleash your potential, you must embrace shared value. This transformative approach to scaling growth aligns your business goals with the needs of your community, creating a win-win for all. Are you ready to join the movement and create a brighter future for Africa?

Shared value: A strategic approach to scaling growth in Africa

The traditional business landscape, which historically focuses solely on profit maximization, is evolving. Shared value offers a compelling approach for businesses seeking to scale excellence. Championed by Harvard professors Michael Porter and Mark Kramer, the concept of shared value recognizes the inherent link between a company's success and the well-being of its surrounding communities (Kramer and Porter, 2011). By proactively addressing social and environmental challenges, our businesses can create economic value while simultaneously generating positive societal impact. This translates into a business strategy that goes beyond simply generating profits. Shared value emphasizes creating economic value in a way that also addresses social needs. Here are some key aspects to consider:

- **Interdependence of success:** Shared value acknowledges the interconnectedness of corporate success and social welfare. You can leverage this by identifying social issues that intersect with your core operations. For instance, a clothing manufacturer in Rwanda could invest in skills development programs, fostering a more skilled local workforce and a more reliable talent pool.

- **Competitive advantage through innovation:** Porter and Kramer posit that addressing social issues can lead to a competitive advantage. Developing innovative solutions for both social and economic challenges can differentiate you in the marketplace.

- **Integration, not separation:** Shared value transcends traditional corporate social responsibility (CSR) initiatives, which are often viewed as separate from core business activities. Instead, shared value emphasizes integrating social and environmental considerations into the very foundation of your strategy and operations.

- **Expanding the value pie:** Shared value aims to create entirely new pools of economic and social value, rather than simply redistributing existing value. It seeks to identify and strengthen the connections between societal progress and economic prosperity.

- **Tangible benefits:** Implementing shared value as part of your core strategy can lead to a multitude of long-term benefits for your company, including increased revenue, reduced costs, a more engaged workforce, and a stronger brand reputation. These advantages occur alongside the positive social and environmental impacts.

In essence, shared value encourages us to view social problems as opportunities for innovation and value creation. It represents a shift toward a more integrated and sustainable approach to business, one that can drive long-term success for our companies while fostering the development of our communities.

The perfect fit for Africa

Now that you understand that shared value is a powerful strategy that still allows you room to dominate the market while making a real difference in Africa, let's dive into why it's the perfect approach for an ambitious business leader like you:

1. **Unlock hidden gems:** Africa is brimming with potential customers, but traditional approaches might miss a huge chunk of the population. Social issues like limited access to finance or underdeveloped infrastructure can create barriers for many. By addressing these challenges, you're not just doing good; you're unlocking entirely new market segments. Imagine creating financial products tailored to the unbanked population or using innovative solutions to bridge the infrastructure gap. These solutions become your gateway to a massive and loyal customer base.

2. **Win hearts and minds:** Africa's youth population is exploding, as within the next decade, more young Africans will be entering the workforce each year than in the rest of the world combined (Mpemba and Munyati, 2023). And guess what? Millennials and Gen

Z prioritize social responsibility. They want to support businesses that share their values. By showcasing your commitment to making a positive impact, you'll build unshakable brand loyalty with this powerful demographic. Think of it as a built-in marketing strategy that resonates deeply with your target audience.

3. **Future-proof your business:** Africa's future is bright, but we must consider environmental challenges. Resource scarcity and climate change are real threats. By taking proactive steps to address these issues, you'll ensure your company thrives in the long run. Imagine being known as an industry leader in eco-friendly practices – that's a competitive advantage money can't buy!

So, you see, shared value isn't just about social good; it's a strategic approach that unlocks unprecedented growth for African businesses. It's about creating a win-win situation for your company and your community. And shared value isn't just a theory – African businesses are already putting it into action with incredible results. Let's look at two inspiring examples that show how shared value can unlock *growth* and *impact*.

LeapFrog Investments: profit with purpose

LeapFrog Investments, a private equity firm partly based in South Africa, champions "profit with purpose."

LeapFrog's shared value approach revolves around investing in sectors that are crucial for Africa's development. The firm focuses on healthcare and financial inclusion – areas where their investments can have a truly transformative impact. By providing capital and expertise to businesses in these sectors, LeapFrog helps them scale and reach more people in need. But LeapFrog also places importance on financial returns, carefully evaluating potential investments for opportunities that offer both strong financial prospects and a positive social impact. This dual focus has helped LeapFrog attract a diverse range of investors, from individuals to institutions.

To measure their success, LeapFrog goes beyond traditional financial metrics, tracking the social impact of their investments by assessing how many people have benefited from their initiatives. For example, they might measure the number of people who have gained financial inclusion or access to affordable healthcare. This data-driven approach allows the firm to demonstrate the tangible results of their work. LeapFrog's successes demonstrate that social good and strong financial performance can go together. They not only make a difference in lives across Africa, but they also generate impressive returns for their investors. By investing in companies that are committed to both profit and purpose, LeapFrog illustrates that a focus on shared value paves the way for a more sustainable and equitable future for the continent.

M-Pesa: banking the unbanked

Safaricom's M-Pesa mobile money platform is a true African shared value success story. It tackled a major social challenge – limited access to traditional banking – and revolutionized the financial landscape. Millions of Africans lacked access to bank accounts and were therefore unable to participate fully in the economy. M-Pesa recognized the critical issue of financial exclusion as an opportunity to address a social problem and build a profit. It built a safe and convenient way for these individuals to send and receive money, pay bills, and even save. According to Safaricom, as of 2017 M-Pesa had enabled over 21 million people in Kenya to access financial services for the first time (Collymore, 2017).

M-Pesa's approach also had a significant impact on businesses. By providing a simple and affordable way to make payments, M-Pesa opened doors for small businesses to participate in the formal economy. This fostered financial inclusion and economic growth, as businesses could now access credit, expand their operations, and create jobs. M-Pesa's success demonstrates the power of shared value innovation to address social needs. It's a win-win for financial inclusion in Africa and a major boost for economic activity.

These are two inspiring examples, but many more African businesses embrace shared value. Shared value represents a powerful paradigm shift for businesses in

Africa. By aligning profit with purpose, our companies can become catalysts for positive change, empowering communities and driving sustainable economic growth. The future of corporate Africa belongs to those who embrace this innovative approach, built on a foundation of shared success!

Collaborating to elevate

Now that you've embraced shared value and understand its power to fuel your business's growth while making a positive impact, let's talk about collaboration. Building a successful African enterprise requires more than just a brilliant idea and relentless hustle. In today's interconnected world, collaboration with diverse partners across sectors and regions has become a critical driver of growth and innovation. Partnerships that bring together complementary skillsets and resources create a synergy that benefits all parties involved. Imagine a data analytics company collaborating with a rural agricultural cooperative. The data company can leverage the cooperative's deep understanding of on-the-ground challenges to develop targeted solutions that improve crop yields. In turn, the cooperative gains access to cutting-edge technology that empowers its members. This collaborative approach fosters innovation while addressing a critical need within the agricultural sector.

When I launched my own pan-African strategy and management consultancy, as the only team member, I was immediately on the lookout for potential strategic partnerships. And with the global network I had built over the years, they were quick to come. The first was with an executive recruiter based in the UK who was looking to expand into the Nigerian market. He had the focus and the process; I had the local contacts and opportunities. Although I had been an HR consultant in a previous life, and could perhaps have done much of what he did myself, I also understood the time commitment that would have taken, distracting me from other areas and initiatives. So, rather than get distracted by the potential loss of revenue, I focused on the leverage and additional value that would come in through the partnership. I have made other strategic partnerships – for example, one with the corporate financial advisory firm featured earlier and another with a niche firm focused on retooling pitch decks – in areas where I may have less experience but that are still very critical to the many SMEs on the continent. Investment readiness, pitching your vision, and the capital-raising and transaction processes are all necessary parts of growth and scale. So I was happy to leverage the power of partnership and bring in others to cover those areas.

The most wonderful thing about my partnerships is how geographically diverse they are. Technology, especially apps like Google and WhatsApp, allows me access to partners based in the USA, Europe, and various countries across Africa. We are building #ZERnation as a community of like-minded individuals who are committed to cultivating a thriving African business landscape through collaboration. But building successful partnerships isn't magic. It requires groundwork. Here are some key practices to keep in mind:

- Before diving in, ensure all parties are aligned on your overall vision and have clearly defined goals for the collaboration. This sets the stage for a smooth journey.

- Africa boasts a vibrant cultural tapestry. Embrace the differences! Foster open and respectful communication, acknowledging cultural nuances and actively listening to your partner's perspective.

- A successful partnership is a two-way street. Ensure the benefits are clearly defined for both parties. What resources, expertise, or market access does each partner bring to the table?

- Outline roles and responsibilities for each partner to avoid confusion and ensure smooth execution.

But where do you find these amazing partners with complementary skills and shared visions? Here's the secret: don't wait until you need them, but rather start building your network of friends and allies now. Think of it as planting seeds – the stronger the network you cultivate, with clarity about your goals and target audience, the more opportunities for collaboration will blossom when the time is right.

Building a network of purpose-driven partners

To find the perfect strategic partners for your business, start building your network now. Networking isn't just about exchanging business cards; it's about forming genuine connections with people who can broaden your perspective. Step outside your comfort zone by attending industry events and exploring events or social gatherings in different sectors. You never know who you might meet! You should also leverage the power of online communities to connect with potential partners across the continent and the globe. Share your expertise by offering to give talks, write guest posts, or participate in online discussions. This will establish you as a thought leader and attract like-minded individuals.

Building strong partnerships requires focus on shared values, time investment, and genuine interest. Look for individuals who resonate with your company's mission and vision. Invest time in understanding their work and offering support. Remember, relationships are two-way streets, so the more you invest in others, the more likely they are to reciprocate. You can also become a connector by identifying potential partnerships between others in your network. This not only strengthens your network but also positions you as a valuable resource. Embracing diversity will spark innovation and expand your reach, as well. Different perspectives can lead to groundbreaking solutions. Understanding cultural nuances ensures smoother collaborations and builds trust.

Maintaining strong networks requires consistency, communication, and cultural sensitivity. Always meet your commitments, keep your network informed, and be mindful of cultural differences. By investing in your network, you contribute to a thriving ecosystem of innovation and shared success. Together, your network can become a powerful force for positive change in the African business landscape.

The power of collaboration

Of course, increased sales figures or expanded market reach are important hallmarks of a successful collaboration. But don't forget the social impact. Did your collaboration create new jobs? Did it empower a local community? Track these metrics alongside traditional business measurements to get a holistic picture. As we've seen, investors are increasingly drawn to businesses that prioritize both financial success and positive social impact. Highlighting the shared value potential of your collaborations can attract valuable investment opportunities.

Collaboration with diverse partners is no longer a luxury, but a strategic imperative for businesses seeking sustainable growth and positive impact. By embracing diverse perspectives, building strong partnerships, and staying on top of emerging trends, you can leverage the power of collaboration to not only propel your business forward but also contribute to the collective growth and prosperity of the African continent. Remember, together we are stronger, and together we can rewrite the rules of the game for African businesses. Let's harness the power of collaboration to build a thriving future for Africa's economic landscape.

Harnessing technology for global collaboration

Technology has revolutionized the way we connect, communicate, and collaborate. In today's interconnected world, it offers your business unprecedented opportunities to expand its reach, forge new partnerships, and drive positive impact. By leveraging technology, you can harness the power of global collaboration to scale your business, reach new markets, and contribute to the development of your community. The same principles behind building a collaborative tribe within your own team apply to external collaboration. Technology can facilitate connections with partners and customers around the world, allowing you to tap into a global network of expertise and resources.

Imagine a time when collaborating with a business partner in South Africa meant hopping on a plane or sending snail mail. Today, thanks to technology, you can connect with them in real time, share documents, and collaborate on projects from the comfort of your own office. This increased accessibility has opened new possibilities for our businesses to partner with international companies, access global markets, and learn from best practices. But technology isn't just about efficiency; it's also about driving social impact. By leveraging digital tools, you can address pressing challenges, create sustainable solutions, and empower marginalized communities. For example, mobile money platforms can provide financial inclusion to underserved populations, while online education platforms can increase access to quality education. To effectively harness the power of technology for global collaboration, you should:

- **Invest in digital infrastructure:** Ensure that your business has access to a reliable internet connection and the necessary hardware and software.

- **Embrace digital tools:** Explore and adopt a range of digital tools that can enhance collaboration, communication, and productivity.

- **Build a strong online presence:** Develop a professional website, maintain an active social media presence, and utilize digital marketing strategies to reach a global audience.

- **Foster a culture of innovation:** Encourage experimentation, creativity, and a willingness to embrace innovative technologies.

- **Prioritize cybersecurity:** Protect your business and customer data by implementing robust cybersecurity measures.

Imagine a small business in rural Kenya struggling to reach customers beyond its local community. With the power of technology, they can set up an online store, connect with customers worldwide, and sell their products to a global audience. Or a social enterprise in Namibia might use mobile technology to provide affordable healthcare to remote villages. These are just two examples of how technology is transforming the African business landscape.

Final thoughts

There's such power in collaboration. By forging strategic partnerships with diverse stakeholders, we can unlock new opportunities, access valuable resources, and address critical challenges. By prioritizing shared value – aligning business goals with the needs of the community – we can create a win-win scenario where both businesses and society thrive. This approach not only enhances our impact but also strengthens our brand reputation and attracts like-minded partners and investors.

Ultimately, the success of our businesses depends on our ability to collaborate effectively. By embracing a spirit of partnership, fostering trust, and leveraging the power of technology, we can build a thriving ecosystem where African businesses flourish, communities prosper, and the continent reaches its full potential.

Conclusion:
You've Got This!

If you've made it this far with me, congratulations! Take a moment to celebrate the journey we've embarked on together. As we turn toward the horizon, I hope you finally understand why I insist on calling myself an Afro-optimist, and perhaps are ready to join me as one yourself. Because what is Afro-optimism anyway, but a mindset? It's a self-assurance, a confident, but not arrogant, attitude that recognizes our accomplishments and talents, inspires us to action and to drive innovation, entrepreneurship, and progress across our beloved continent. Afro-optimism is not blind positivity. It's a nuanced perspective that acknowledges the beauty and potential of Africa, while remaining clear-eyed about the challenges we face. It's the recognition of individual and collective accomplishments alongside the understanding that there are obstacles to overcome. This optimism is the fuel that propels our action, innovation, and enterprising spirit, driving us forward toward a brighter future.

The philosophy of Afro-optimism transcends borders. I, a global Nigerian with an American accent, a German mind, and a Nigerian heart, embody this spirit. Afro-optimism is about showcasing our excellence as Africans under a united front that celebrates individual brilliance while recognizing the power of collective action. This excellence is rooted in a deep desire to serve our communities. It's about finding ingenious solutions with limited resources and building social good with a sustainable impact for generations to come.

Our journey as Afro-optimists has been a continuous learning experience. Through ethical leadership, the creation of dream teams, and navigating the complexities of regulations, we've transformed crises into opportunities to build African excellence. We've discovered that leadership isn't a top-down decree, but about creating a culture of accountability, communication, and transparency – essential elements of the SCALE framework. We've learned to leverage challenges, gaining a competitive edge by unlocking new markets and building trust with all our stakeholders. By *Strategizing* our approach, *Championing* our team, *Accelerating* our leadership, *Leveraging* our governance, and *Expanding* our reach, we can overcome any obstacle and continue to contribute to the growth and prosperity of Africa. This kind of leadership fosters trust – the bedrock of any thriving organization. We've also come to understand that we can only achieve this trust with the right people. We need a passionate tribe that shares our vision for Africa's future. This shared purpose can propel us through fluctuating currencies, infrastructural gaps, and murky regulations that sometimes impede progress.

Afro-optimism is our superpower as leaders. It's a unique blend of resilience, resourcefulness, and unwavering belief that allows us to thrive in the face of adversity. It calls us to embrace our own strengths, to develop a strategic hustle that prioritizes sustainable models, empower our people, and learn from failures. As Afro-optimists, we aren't afraid to fall, because we know we can use setbacks as springboards for innovation. There will be bumps along the road, but we embrace them as opportunities to learn, adapt, and innovate. We leverage our local knowledge as a powerful asset that sets us apart from the competition. This is how we harness the power of Afro-optimism, not just to build successful businesses in Africa, but to forge a brighter future for our beloved continent.

But our journey doesn't end here. We must become storytellers, sharing our successes and challenges to inspire others. Let's become mentors, nurturing the next generation of Afro-optimists who will take the reins and push the boundaries of what's possible. Together, as Afro-optimists, we can turn dreams into reality. Let's go forth and inspire others to join us on this incredible journey. As we move forward, let Afro-optimism be the guiding light that illuminates our path toward a prosperous and vibrant Africa.

Paying it forward

Just the other day, I was sitting on an interview panel for one of my clients, who was looking for a senior executive. We had two quite interesting final candidates to assess. At the end of each hour-long session, we naturally allowed the candidates the opportunity to ask us any questions. At one point, one of my fellow interviewers turned to me and commented, "It's as if she's interviewing you!" I smiled, but I hadn't even noticed, because I've encountered people's curiosity about my journey so often, and I am usually happy to oblige. I understand the reason for all the questions and relish the opportunity to provide the same casual mentoring that I myself received over the years. I understand my duty to pass that same access on to others, with only one request: pay it forward.

One of my favorite ways to pay it forward is mentorship. Although it always came naturally to me as a consultant, mentorship is more than just giving advice; it's fostering a supportive community where aspiring entrepreneurs can thrive. I'm always happy to share my experiences – both the successes and, especially, the challenges. I want you to know that your vulnerability will inspire others and normalize the inevitable setbacks that come with building a business. Your mentorship can be a one-off encounter, as in the situation with the interview, or part of a formal mentorship program that connects experienced entrepreneurs with budding go-getters.

Every so often, I come across someone, through a random social media post or in-person run-in, who claims me as their mentor, although we've never met. They may follow me on LinkedIn, or they may have seen me speak somewhere or encountered former colleagues of mine. While I haven't fully deduced what this might mean, it does highlight for me the valuable guidance we can provide to those who might not otherwise have access to it. That's why we, at ZER Consulting Africa (ZER), created the #ZERnation community on WhatsApp to share learning tidbits. It's why we provide free online resources via our online learning center, showcasing webinars, video tutorials, and downloadable toolkits that both current and aspiring entrepreneurs can access on their own schedule. In addition to incorporating shared value within our business strategy, we actively align our company's mission with specific SDGs, attracting like-minded talent, customers, and investors who share our values. This also fosters a sense of purpose and pride within our team, leading to increased innovation and productivity. Taking it a step further, in the future we plan to partner with other entrepreneurs and organizations to amplify our social impact. Collectively, we can tackle larger challenges and create a more sustainable future for Africa.

By paying it forward, we, as business leaders, build a robust ecosystem where Afro-optimism flourishes. Together, we can nurture a generation of entrepreneurs who will transform Africa's future. Remember, the success of one entrepreneur strengthens the entire continent. Let's create a legacy of shared knowledge, unwavering support, and relentless pursuit of progress. This is the true embodiment of Afro-optimism in action.

We can extend this concept even further by fostering a culture of collaboration within the African entrepreneurial community. Imagine a network where entrepreneurs from different countries and industries can share best practices, resources, and even potential business partnerships. This kind of collaboration can accelerate innovation and create a multiplier effect for success across the continent, which is exactly ZER's intention with #ZERnation. Our legacy is more than just our business. When we empower others, we create a ripple effect that extends far beyond our immediate sphere. Encouraging our mentees to pay it forward creates a sustainable cycle of support and growth.

Leaving our mark

I hope you've devoured these pages, inspired by the stories of resilience, innovation, and leadership that paint a vibrant portrait of a rising Africa. Now, I hope a collective fire burns within you – the entrepreneurial spirit urging you to contribute. The question resonates: How can you leave your mark on this vibrant continent and the world? The answer lies in building businesses that embody Afro-optimism and shape Africa's future, businesses that aren't just about financial success but also about fusing social impact, cultural pride, and the empowerment of future generations.

Amid the vibrant chaos in the bustling market in Accra, Ghana, I met Ama, a young entrepreneur brimming with innovative ideas but struggling to secure funding. Her dream of sustainable tote bags empowering local artisans resonated deeply with me. Fast-forward a few years, and with our collaboration, Ama's company could become a global phenomenon – a testament to the transformative power of mentorship and Afro-optimism.

When, together, we develop comprehensive growth strategies aligned with our vision and values, build a high-performing team that shares our passion for Africa's development, navigate the complexities of the African business environment with expert guidance, and measure and maximize our social impact alongside financial success, we can unleash the full potential of African entrepreneurship and create a brighter future for our continent. **Success goes beyond the bottom line.** It's the story etched not just in financial statements but in the lives we touch and the communities we uplift.

Expanding our impact

Legacy isn't built alone. We can each invest in young businesses by considering angel investing or venture capital opportunities that support promising African startups. And our impact extends beyond just finances. We can each offer expertise and mentorship to the leaders of these young companies, helping them navigate the challenges we've already overcome. We can all use our collective voice to influence policymakers and decision-makers. Partnering with industry organizations or NGOs amplifies our advocacy efforts, lobbying for policies that encourage entrepreneurship and address challenges faced by African businesses. Together, we can create a ripple effect that extends beyond our companies. We can advocate for opportunities for underrepresented groups to participate in the entrepreneurial ecosystem. This might involve providing scholarships or grants specifically for female entrepreneurs or entrepreneurs from minority groups, or organizing workshops that address the unique challenges faced by these groups.

Leaving our mark is not about owning individual spaces, but about joining a chorus of voices amplifying the power and potential of Africa. Let's work together to make our businesses forces for good, testaments to the collective spirit of Ubuntu. Together, we can rewrite the narrative, turning Afro-optimism from a philosophy to a reality – part of a continent on the rise, where success is measured not just in profits, but in the positive transformation it leaves behind. Embrace your responsibility, unleash your creativity, and go forth to leave your mark on an Africa poised to inspire the world. That's the vision of the Afro-optimist.

To learn more about #ZERnation and join an open and vibrant community of Afro-optimists transforming Africa's future, visit zerconsulting.com. And if you haven't yet done so, now's your chance to complete our SCALE scorecard at https://zerconsulting.com /scaleyourbusiness and start building your legacy of excellence.

References

African Union (n.d.) "The diaspora division" [online]. Available at: https://au.int/en/diaspora-division (accessed November 21, 2024)

African Union (2018) "Summary of the key decisions and declarations of the 31st African Union Summit," July 6 [online]. Available at: https://au.int/en/pressreleases/20180706/summary-key-decisions-and-declarations-31st-african-union-summit (accessed November 21, 2024)

Bennet, J. (1998) "The testing of a president: The visitor; Mandela, at White House, says world backs Clinton," *New York Times*, September 23 [online]. Available at: www.nytimes.com/1998/09/23/us/testing-president-visitor-mandela-white-house-says-world-backs-clinton.html (accessed November 21, 2024)

Clance, P.R. and Imes, S.A. (1978) "The imposter phenomenon in high achieving women: Dynamics and therapeutic intervention," *Psychotherapy: Theory, Research & Practice*, 15(3), 241–247, https://doi.org/10.1037/h0086006 (accessed December 13, 2024)

Collymore, B. (2017) "Mobile money: Africa's force for social good," Safaricom Newsroom, April 8 [online]. Available at: https://newsroom.safaricom.co.ke/innovation/mobile-money-africas-force-for-social-good/ (accessed November 21, 2024)

Fawry (n.d.) "About" [online]. Available at: www.fawry.com/about (accessed November 21, 2024)

Frangoul, A. (2015) "Pay-as-you-go solar power takes off in Africa," CNBC, February 25 [online]. Available at: www.cnbc.com/2015/02/25/pay-as-you-go-solar-power-takes-off-in-africa.html (accessed November 21, 2024)

Fujikawa, J. (2018) "Welcome to Wakanda: Everything you need to know about *Black Panther* before you get to the theater," Marvel, February 14 [online]. Available at: www.marvel.com/articles/movies/welcome-to-wakanda-everything-you-need-to-know-about-black-panther-before-you-get-to-the-theater (accessed November 21, 2024)

IOM Regional Office for West and Central Africa (2023) "Harnessing the potential of the Ghanaian diaspora for national development: Coordinated efforts needed," November 2 [online]. Available

at: https://rodakar.iom.int/news/harnessing
-potential-ghanaian-diaspora-national-development
-coordinated-efforts-needed (accessed December 13,
2024)

Jumia (n.d.) "About us" [online]. Available at: www
.jumia.co.ke/fragment/contents/sp-about_new/?lang=
en#anchistory (accessed November 21, 2024)

Jumia (n.d.) "Our company" [online]. Available at:
https://investor.jumia.com/our-company/default
.aspx (accessed November 21, 2024)

Keller, G., with Papasan J. (2013) *The ONE Thing: The
surprisingly simple truth behind extraordinary results.* La
Vergne, TN: Bard Press

LeapFrog Investments (n.d.) "How we invest"
[online]. Available at: https://leapfroginvest.com
/how-we-invest (accessed November 21, 2024)

LeapFrog Investments (n.d.) "Impact measurement"
[online]. Available at: https://leapfroginvest.com/our
-impact (accessed November 21, 2024)

Mpemba, C. and Munyati, C. (2023) "How Africa's
youth will drive global growth" August 16 [online].
Available at: www.weforum.org/stories/2023/08
/africa-youth-global-growth-digital-economy
(accessed December 13, 2024)

Ngozi Adichie, C. (2009) "The danger of a single story," TEDGlobal, July [online]. Available at: www.ted.com/talks/chimamanda_ngozi_adichie_the_danger_of_a_single_story (accessed November 21, 2024)

Nicols, B. (2021) "Are you an imposter?" The InnovateMR Blog, April 16 [online]. Available at: www.innovatemr.com/insights/are-you-an-imposter (accessed November 21, 2024)

Porter, M.E. and Kramer, M. (2011) *Creating shared value: How to reinvent capitalism – and unleash a wave of innovation and growth," Harvard Business Review*, January–February [online]. Available at: https://hbr.org/2011/01/the-big-idea-creating-shared-value (accessed November 21, 2024)

State of the African Diaspora (SOAD) (n.d.) "The African diaspora" [online]. Available at: https://thestateofafricandiaspora.com/the-african-diaspora (accessed December 13, 2024)

The Diaspora Affairs, Office of the President (DAOOP) [online]. Available at: https://diasporaaffairs.gov.gh (accessed December 13, 2024)

The Diaspora Collective (2019) "African diaspora: A global impact" [online]. Available at: https://thediasporacollective.com/blogs/discover/the-african-diaspora (accessed December 13, 2024)

World Bank Group (2022) "Free trade deal boosts Africa's economic development," June 30 [online]. Available at: www.worldbank.org/en/topic/trade/publication/free-trade-deal-boosts-africa-economic-development (accessed December 13, 2024)

Further Reading

Below is a curated list of further reading suggestions, with one book recommended for each month of the year, so you can deepen your understanding of the concepts and topics explored in this book.

Ash, M.K., *The Mary Kay Way: Timeless principles from America's greatest woman entrepreneur* (Wiley, 2009)

Offers timeless entrepreneurial wisdom for African CEOs, highlighting the power of a people-first approach in creating a supportive ecosystem for growth and success.

Harrington, K. and Priestley, D., *Key Person of Influence: The five-step method to become one of the most highly valued and highly paid people in your industry* (Rethink Press, 2015)

Outlines a five-step method for becoming a highly valued and highly paid expert in your field, whether in Africa or beyond. Emphasizes building a strong personal brand, establishing yourself as a thought leader, and leveraging your network to attract opportunities.

Hilimire, J., *The 5-Day Turnaround: Be the leader you always wanted to be* (Ripples Media, 2019)

Teaches leaders how to embrace a startup mentality and drive transformative growth. Hilimire's practical strategies and actionable insights can equip African leaders with the tools to turn around their organizations and foster a culture of innovation and agility.

Horowitz, B., *The Hard Thing About Hard Things: building a business when there are no easy answers* (Harper Business, 2014)

Presents a brutally honest guide to building a successful business, focusing on the challenges and difficult decisions often overlooked in other business books. Should resonate with African entrepreneurs who seek a no-nonsense approach to tackling the complexities of business leadership on the continent.

Keller, G. with Papasan, J., *The ONE Thing: The surprisingly simple truth behind extraordinary results* (Bard Press, 2013)

Emphasizes the power of focus and prioritization, arguing that extraordinary results stem from identifying and relentlessly pursuing your most important task. This must be our mindset for harnessing Africa's potential through targeted action and strategic prioritization.

Lafley, A.G. and Martin, R.L., *Playing to Win: How strategy really works* (Harvard Business Review Press, 2013)

Provides a strategic framework for businesses to achieve sustainable success. Its principles of strategic clarity and disciplined execution can be invaluable for African entrepreneurs and leaders seeking to scale their businesses and compete on the global stage.

Miller, R., *Be Chief: It's a choice, not a title*, 2nd edition (independently published, 2023)

Challenges the notion that leadership is reserved for those with formal titles. Empowers individuals at all levels to embrace their inner "chief" and drive positive change within their organization. Encourages individuals to take ownership of their careers and contribute to Africa's growth.

Peterson, D., Lochhead, C. and Maney, K., *Play Bigger: How pirates, dreamers, and innovators create and dominate markets* (Harper Business, 2016)

Introduces the concept of category design, which involves creating new market categories and dominating them. By defining their own unique value propositions and building strong brands, African businesses can establish themselves as leaders in their respective fields.

Randolph, M., *That Will Never Work: The birth of Netflix by the first CEO and co-founder Marc Randolph* (Little, Brown and Company, 2019)

Recounts Netflix's unconventional journey, in which Randolph and his team persevered, fueled by a belief in their vision, despite facing skepticism and industry resistance. Highlights the importance of defying expectations, embracing innovation, and building a culture of resilience.

Sinek, S., *Start with Why: How leaders inspire everyone to take action* (Portfolio, 2011)

Explores the power of purpose-driven leadership, arguing that successful leaders and organizations inspire people by starting with their "why" – their core beliefs and motivations. The Afro-optimist mindset also emphasizes the importance of having a strong sense of purpose and vision for Africa's future.

Stanier, M.B., *The Coaching Habit: Say less, ask more and change the way you lead forever* (Page Two, 2016)

Teaches leaders how to unlock their team's potential by asking powerful questions instead of giving orders. This approach fosters a culture of empowerment and innovation, demonstrating how we can unlock Africa's potential through leadership excellence.

Wallace, W.T., *You Can't Know It All: Leading in the age of deep expertise* (Harper Business, 2019)

Argues that in today's complex world, leaders must shift from relying solely on their own expertise to empowering and trusting their teams. This resonates with our emphasis on the importance of building a champion team that shares your drive and passion.

Acknowledgments

I am deeply grateful to the many individuals and organizations who have supported me on this journey. Without your encouragement, guidance, and love, *Afro-Optimism Unleashed* would not have been possible.

To Daddy – your unwavering love and encouragement have been my constant source of strength.

To my husband Hakan, my children Deniz Adeola and Batu Adekola, my second mother Auntie Biodun, and the rest of my very beloved and very extended African family, including all my "aunties," "uncles," and "cousins," and especially to all who came before me – thanks for believing in and supporting my vision for my life.

To all my dear friends worldwide who have welcomed me from country to country – thank you for becoming my second family, with your countless hours of listening to, laughing with, and inspiring me.

To the incredible ZER team – your dedication, expertise, and unwavering support have been invaluable.

To Seun and Matt – your insights and contributions have significantly enriched this book.

To my beta readers, Andrew, Bode, Derrick, Ibrahim, Kanini, Marsha, Sylvester, and Tiekie – your honest feedback and encouragement have been invaluable.

To the Rethink Press teams – thank you for your professionalism, guidance, and belief in this project.

To my mentors and advisers over the years – your wisdom, support, and mentorship have shaped my thinking and inspired my journey.

To the organizations and communities that have shaped me, State College Area School District, the Pennsylvania State University, the African Students Association, and the countless others – thank you for nurturing my growth.

To the late Pastor Grabill – your early words of weekly wisdom helped set me on the right path.

Finally, to all the inspirational figures who have paved the way for African excellence – your legacy continues to inspire us all.

Thank you to everyone who has contributed to this book. Your support means the world to me.

The Author

Renowned Afro-optimist Adeolu Adewumi-Zer has been a global strategist and champion of African excellence for over twenty-five years. As the founder of ZER Consulting Africa, she empowers leaders and businesses across the continent to achieve sustainable growth and impact.

Having spearheaded strategic growth initiatives across Africa, before leading a major financial institution in Nigeria, Adeolu's strategic insights and unwavering commitment to excellence have earned her numerous accolades. A mother of two global Africans, her Afro-optimism extends beyond business as she advocates for financial inclusion, gender equality, and quality education.

Are you an entrepreneur, CEO, or an Afro-optimist? Join the #ZERnation movement! Grab your copy and connect with Adeolu:

🌐 https://zerconsulting.com

in https://linkedin.com/in/adeoluadewumi

www.ingramcontent.com/pod-product-compliance
Ingram Content Group UK Ltd.
Pitfield, Milton Keynes, MK11 3LW, UK
UKHW031848100225
454922UK00010B/156